Judge for Yourself

Judge for Yourself

Famous American Trials for Readers Theatre

Suzanne I. Barchers

TEACHER IDEAS PRESS
Portsmouth, NH

Teacher Ideas Press
A division of Reed Elsevier Inc.
361 Hanover Street
Portsmouth, NH 03801-3912
www.teacherideaspress.com

Offices and agents throughout the world

© 2004 by Suzanne I. Barchers

All rights reserved. No part of this book may be reproduced in any form or by any electronic or mechanical means, including information storage and retrieval systems, without permission in writing from the publisher, except by a reviewer, who may quote brief passages in a review. An exception is made for individual librarians and educators who may make copies of the scripts for classroom use. Reproducible pages may be copied for classroom and educational programs only. Performance may be videotaped for school or library purposes.

The author and publisher wish to thank those who have generously given permission to reprint borrowed material:

Photos of John Wilkes Booth, Susan B. Anthony, Lizzie Bordon, Joe Jackson, the Leopold and Leob Trial, John T. Scopes, Al Capone, and the Lindbergh Trial are reprinted by permission of AP/Wide World Photo.

Photo of David C. Stephenson is reprinted by permission of Corbis Corporation. Copyright © Bettmann/CORBIS.

Photo of Ossian Sweet is used courtesy of the Burton Historical Collection, Detroit Public Library.

Library of Congress Cataloging-in-Publication Data
Barchers, Suzanne I.
   Judge for yourself : famous American trials for readers theatre /
Suzanne I. Barchers.
      p.   cm.
Includes bibliographical references.
  ISBN 1-56308-959-9
 1.   Trials—United States.   I. Title.
KF220.B37   2003
345.73'07—dc22   2003021777

Editor: Barbara Ittner
Production Coordinator: Angela Laughlin
Typesetter: Westchester Book Services
Cover design: Gaile Ivaska
Manufacturing: Steve Bernier

Printed in the United States of America on acid-free paper

08 07 06 05 04 ML 1 2 3 4 5

Dedicated to Josh and Jen Barchers, who always show good judgment.

Contents

Introduction ix

1. A Deadly Secret 1
   The Lincoln Assassination Conspiracy Trial

2. A Woman's Right 13
   The United States vs. Susan B. Anthony

3. She Took an Axe 25
   The Commonwealth of Massachusetts vs. Lizzie Borden

4. "Say It Ain't So" 43
   The State of Illinois vs. Eddie Cicotte et al.:
   The White Sox Scandal of 1919

5. A Perfect Crime 59
   The People against Nathan Leopold, Jr. and Richard Loeb:
   The Sentencing Hearing

6. Taking the Test 71
   The State of Tennessee vs. John Thomas Scopes:
   The Scopes Monkey Trial

7. An Arrogant Man 89
   The Trial of David C. Stephenson, Grand Dragon
   of the Ku Klux Klan

8. In Defense of Home 103
   The People of Michigan vs. Ossian Sweet et al.

9. Evading the Truth 117
   The United States of America vs. Al Capone

10. When the Bough Breaks **135**
The State vs. Hauptmann: The Trial of Bruno Richard Hauptmann for the Kidnapping and Murder of Charles A. Lindbergh, Jr.

Bibliography	**155**
Title Index	**157**
About the Author	**159**

Introduction

People are fascinated with our judicial system. From fictional television series such as "Law and Order" and "The Practice" to daytime shows such as "Judge Judy" to televised trials of people accused of a variety of crimes, viewers can't seem to get enough of trials. Famous trials from the past—from the Scopes Monkey trial to Al Capone's trial—are equally captivating, providing a glimpse into history. *Judge for Yourself: Famous American Trials for Readers Theatre* includes ten scripts representing nine trials and one hearing that had significant impact or far-reaching implications. For example, many students may be aware that Susan B. Anthony was a famous suffragette, but few may be aware that she was on trial for trying to vote. Students may be familiar with the controversy surrounding the teaching of evolution in school, but will many know that the town leaders of Dayton, Tennessee actively decided to seek out this court case to foster tourism in their town?

Reading these trials is just the beginning of the opportunities for drawing parallels to recent or current events. Readers may note a disturbing parallel between the Leopold and Loeb case, in which a fourteen-year-old boy is marked for a random death, and drive-by shootings. The trial of Al Capone for income tax evasion will undoubtedly remind students of corporate executives or famous celebrities who have been investigated for insider stock trading. After reading the trial about Lizzie Borden, readers may speculate as to whether both she and O. J. Simpson got away with murder.

Librarians and teachers will find that using these scripts of landmark trials provides the ideal opportunity to enhance the history, social studies, humanities, or English program in a lively fashion.

HOW THE TRIALS WERE CHOSEN

When researching this book, it was challenging to decide which trials to include. Some trials, such as the Scopes Monkey trial and the trial prompted by Susan B. Anthony's attempt to vote, were obvious choices because of their landmark decisions. Other trials, such as Lizzie Borden's and Al Capone's, were chosen because of the compelling—and admittedly scandalous—stories behind each trial. The trial in which Ossian Sweet and his relatives were charged with murder may be less familiar, however, the issue of racial integration and defense of one's home and neighborhood against threat—or change—continues to be of interest. Although other trials were important historically, some were not included because of the complexity of the trial, the extensive testimony, or because the trial's relevance would be less obvious without a rich background in the history and culture of the time period.

DEVELOPING THE TRIALS

The books used for background information are listed with each trial. In addition original transcripts of most of these trials were consulted, and they proved to be an invaluable source of information. Complete transcripts for most of these and other trials can be found at http://www.law.umkc.edu/faculty/projects/ftrials/ftrials.htm. In some cases, such as the trial of the eight White Sox team members, characters begin telling the story long before the trial. These conversations may be based on a variety of sources such as newspaper articles and trial transcripts. In other cases, the conversations, such as those between Eliot Ness and his mother, Emma Ness, in the script about Al Capone, though based on research about the characters, are more imaginative.

Just as they do today, important trials could last weeks, producing hundreds of pages of testimony. Therefore it was necessary to review the testimony to determine what might be included to provide an interesting case. Whenever possible, a balance of key points from both the prosecution and the defense were included so that the script could be stopped when the jury would be deliberating the verdict, allowing students or the audience to wrestle with the judgment. It should be noted that some trials, such as the trial of Bruno Richard Hauptmann for the kidnapping and murder of Charles A. Lindbergh, Jr., seem to unfold in a one-sided fashion. In this case, many books have been written containing theories about the truth, with many emphasizing that the popularity and celebrity status of Charles A. Lindbergh put tremendous pressure on the police to find the murderer. For this script, the story unfolds through trial testimony. Students may want to read about other theories of what might have happened the night the baby disappeared and debate whether Hauptmann was unjustly convicted and executed.

Although every effort was made to maintain the tone of each character, it was usually necessary to condense much of the testimony into manageable segments. Some significant portions of famous opening statements and summations are included verbatim, especially important excerpts from famous attorneys such as Clarence Darrow. In the case of the trial of Lizzie Borden, representative testimony was pieced together from a variety of secondary sources.

USING READERS THEATRE

Readers theatre can be compared to radio plays. Rather than on a dramatic, memorized presentation, the emphasis is on an effective reading of the script. Reading orally develops strong reading skills, and listening to scripts promotes active listening for people in the audience. In addition, the scripts provide educators with an opportunity for preparing a special program, for introducing a new area of study, or for a diversion from the regular curriculum.

Preparing the Scripts

Preread any trial before using it in the classroom, keeping the maturity of your students in mind. The trial of David C. Stephenson was included because of the role of the Ku Klux

Klan in the United States at that time. Although this trial deals with Stephenson's brutal rape of a young woman as tactfully as possible, some teachers or students may find the topic uncomfortable. In spite of the adaptations of the testimony, the language of some characters in these scripts may seem stilted or wordy, and students can be encouraged to paraphrase. In some scripts, the attorneys have long passages and students should rehearse carefully these lines in particular.

Once scripts are chosen for reading, make enough copies for all of the characters, plus an extra set or two for your use and a replacement copy. To help readers keep their place, have participants use highlighter markers to designate their character's role within the copy. For example, someone reading the role of Narrator 1 could highlight his or her lines in blue, with another character highlighting his or her lines in yellow.

Photocopied scripts will last longer if you use a three-hole punch (or copy them on pre-punched paper) and place them in inexpensive folders. The folders can be color-coordinated with the internal highlighting for each character's part. The title of the play can be printed on the outside of the folder, and scripts can be stored easily for the next reading. This preparation of the scripts is a good project for a student aide or volunteer parent. It takes a minimum of initial attention and needs to be repeated only when a folder is lost.

Getting Started

For the first experience with a readers theatre script, consider choosing a short story or a script with many characters to involve more readers. Gather the readers informally. Next, introduce the script and explain that readers theatre does not mean memorizing a play and acting it out, but rather reading a script aloud, perhaps with a few props and actions. Select volunteers to do the initial reading, allowing them an opportunity to review silently their parts before reading aloud. Be sure that the students who will be part of the jury or audience do not have an opportunity to hear the verdict prior to making their judgment. (If they are already familiar with the trial and outcome, encourage the students to consider justifying an alternative verdict in performance.) Discuss definitions or pronunciations of challenging words as necessary. While these readers are preparing to read their script, another group can brainstorm ideas for props or staging, if appropriate.

Before reading the first script, decide whether to choose parts after the reading or to introduce additional scripts to involve more participants. If readers are reading scripts based on several trials, a readers theatre workshop could be held, with each student belonging to a group that prepares a script for presentation. A readers theatre festival could be planned for a special day when several short scripts are presented consecutively, with brief intermissions between each reading.

Once the participants have read the scripts and become familiar with the new vocabulary, determine which readers will read the various parts. Some parts are considerably more demanding than others, and readers should be encouraged to volunteer for roles that will be comfortable. Once they are familiar with readers theatre, readers should try a reading that is more challenging. Reading scripts is especially useful for remedial reading students. The adaptation is often written in simpler language with little description, giving readers an easier version of the story. Reading orally also serves to improve silent reading skills. However, it is equally important that the readers enjoy the literature.

Presentation Suggestions

In readers theatre, readers traditionally stand—or sit on stools, chairs, or the floor—in a formal presentation style. The narrators may stand with the scripts placed on music stands or lecterns slightly off to one or both sides. The readers may hold their scripts in black or colored folders.

Presentation suggestions often indicate having the characters placed with the prosecution or the defense. The judge might sit on a high stool above other characters. Minor characters could leave the stage after their reading. For a long script with many main characters, the characters could sit informally on a variety of chairs. The scripts include a few suggestions for positioning readers, but participants should be encouraged to create interesting arrangements.

In many of the scripts in this collection, there are few female roles. Remind students that they are acting and that it is appropriate for a female to read a male part. Encourage the students to recast the attorneys' roles as women.

Props

Traditional readers theatre has few props, if any. However, simple costuming effects, such as clothes of the period, plus a few props on stage will lend interest to the presentation. Readers should be encouraged to decide how much to add to their reading. For some readers, the use of props or actions may be distracting, and the emphasis should remain on the reading rather than on an overly complicated presentation.

Delivery Suggestions

It is important to discuss with the readers ways to enliven the scripts orally as they read. During their first experiences with presenting a script, readers are often tempted to keep their heads buried in the script, making sure they don't miss a line. However, readers can and should learn the material well enough to look up from the script during the presentation. Readers can also learn to use onstage focus—to look at each other during the presentation. This is most logical for characters that are interacting with each other. The use of offstage focus—the presenters look directly into the eyes of the audience—is more logical for the narrator of characters who are uninvolved with onstage characters. Alternatively, have readers who do not interact with each other focus on a prearranged offstage location, such as the classroom clock, during delivery. Simple actions, such as gestures or turning, can also be incorporated into readers theatre.

Generally the audience should be able to see the readers' facial expressions during the reading. Upon occasion, it might seem logical for a character, such as an attorney, to move across the stage, facing another character while reading. In this event, the characters should be turned enough so that the audience can see the reader's face.

The Next Steps

Once readers have enjoyed the reading process involved in preparing and presenting readers theatre, students may want to conduct further research. More information, such as photographs, artifacts, and additional trial transcripts, can be found on the Internet. Consider having students write scenes using other testimony or evidence. Students can rewrite closing arguments in an attempt to strengthen a prosecution or a defense. Students can prepare an appeal, write a script that details the jury's deliberations, or prepare arguments for the sentencing hearing.

To practice summarization skills, students can develop mock television or radio reports of the proceedings, write newspaper trial accounts or editorials, or write profiles of various characters. Students can hone their research and oral skills by debating topics such as the death penalty. Finally, challenge students to create their own scripts. Students can review http://www.law.umkc.edu/faculty/projects/ftrials/ftrials.htm for other trial possibilities. Encourage writers to choose trials with compelling stories and to explore how they can weave in the story through fictional characters. Remember that the primary purpose of using readers theatre is to enhance the curriculum. Curtain's up!

1

A Deadly Secret

The Lincoln Assassination Conspiracy Trial

John Wilkes Booth, assassin of President Abraham Lincoln. AP Photo/Sun Classic Pictures, Inc.

INTRODUCTION

After the assassination of President Abraham Lincoln on April 14, 1865, the government moved quickly to track down various alleged conspirators. John Wilkes Booth, the assassin, vowed to die before being captured. Indeed, he was shot and killed on April 26 at Garrett's farm in Virginia, where he was hiding. But did Booth act alone, or was he part of a conspiracy? Seven men and one woman were arrested and charged with conspiring to assassinate Lincoln. They were tried by a military commission, rather than by a civilian court, based on the reasoning that the city of Washington remained under martial law. Eleven members of the commission heard testimony from more than 350 witnesses during six weeks. The majority of the witnesses were called in the prosecution and defense of Mary Surratt and Dr. Samuel Mudd, whose guilt remains in dispute to this day. (The phrase "your name is mud" derives from the stigma attached to Dr. Mudd's conviction. At the time of the printing of this book, the family of Dr. Samuel Mudd continues their efforts to clear his name.) Because there were so many members on the commission, in this script there is one prosecuting attorney used in generic fashion. In contrast to other scripts in this collection, the outcome is provided and participants are urged to consider whether there was a conspiracy.

PRESENTATION SUGGESTIONS

Students can dress in clothing or use accessories (e.g., stovepipe hats, long skirts) of the time period—late nineteenth century. The witnesses can sit on one side of the stage, with Lincoln, the narrators, and other characters on the other side of the stage. Students can research military and presidential symbols of the time and decorate the stage if desired.

RELATED BOOK

Hanchett, William. *The Lincoln Murder Conspiracies.* Urbana and Chicago: University of Illinois Press, 1983.

THE LINCOLN ASSASSINATION CONSPIRACY TRIAL

CHARACTERS

Narrator 1

Narrator 2

Ward Hill Lamon, *friend of Abraham Lincoln*

Abraham Lincoln, *President of the United States*

John Wilkes Booth, *assassin*

Edwin Booth, *John Wilkes Booth's brother*

Asia Booth, *John Wilkes Booth's sister*

Samuel B. Arnold, *accused conspirator*

Michael O'Laughlin, *accused conspirator*

Lewis Payne, *accused conspirator*

James P. Ferguson, *restaurant proprietor and witness*

Prosecuting Attorney

Joseph Burroughs, *witness and employee at Ford Theatre*

John M. Lloyd, *witness and resident at Mrs. Surratt's tavern*

Louis J. Weichmann, *witness and resident at Mrs. Surratt's tavern*

Defense Attorney

R. C. Morgan, *witness and employee at the War Department*

J. Z. Jenkins, *witness and acquaintance of Mrs. Surratt*

Jacob Ritterspaugh, *witness and acquaintance of Edward Spangler*

William H. Bell, *witness and a servant in the home of Secretary of State William Seward*

Sergeant George F. Robinson, *attendant to Secretary of State Seward*

Colonel Henry H. Wells, *witness and interrorgator of Samuel Mudd*

A Deadly Secret

The Lincoln Assassination Conspiracy Trial

Scene 1

Narrator 1: Ever since Abraham Lincoln was first elected U.S. President in 1860, there were people who threatened to strike a "deadly blow" against him. During the next few years, and over the tumultuous years of the Civil War, thousands of angry letters directed at the president arrive at the White House. A secretary discards most of them after a quick reading.

Narrator 2: Ward Hill Lamon, an old friend and legal associate from Danville who often carries two revolvers and a bowie knife as he accompanies Lincoln in public, tries to warn the president of the danger.

Ward Hill Lamon: Mr. President, you need to be more careful in crowds. We keep hearing rumors of assassins.

Abraham Lincoln: I cannot be shut up in an iron cage and guarded!

Ward Hill Lamon: You can't ignore all the angry letters, Abe.

Abraham Lincoln: I don't take those seriously. Do you think anyone who wants to kill me is going to write and tell me first? Not hardly!

Ward Hill Lamon: Still, I wish you would show a bit more care.

Abraham Lincoln: You worry too much.

Narrator 1: During the summer, Lincoln often visits the Soldiers' Home founded for Mexican War Veterans. The home in the country is cool and pleasant. One August evening, Lincoln rides along the woods at the edge of the grounds, deep in thought. Suddenly a bullet from a rifle speeds past his head. He rides back to the home where Lamon waits.

Abraham Lincoln: Ward! There's someone out there with a rifle. A bullet whizzed right by me!

Ward Hill Lamon: Are you okay?

Abraham Lincoln: Yes, yes. It was probably just an accident.

Ward Hill Lamon: At this time of night? I don't think so.

Narrator 2: By 1863, Lincoln accepts the need to have a military escort when he goes to the Soldiers' Home. Armed guards patrol the White House. By the time Lincoln is reelected in 1864, he resigns himself to using an official bodyguard whenever he takes a walk.

Scene 2

Narrator 1: There is one man who especially despises Lincoln. John Wilkes Booth enjoys an affluent Southern lifestyle. Like his father, who had died in 1821, Booth is a talented actor. John often has heated political discussions with his brother, Edwin, and his sister, Asia.

John Wilkes Booth: Edwin, I don't understand how you can support this Union nonsense.

Edwin Booth: What would you suggest, John? Lincoln is getting what he wants.

John Wilkes Booth: I'll tell you what I suggest! We need to find a way to get rid of him.

Asia Booth: The President? Hush, John. Don't carry on like that.

John Wilkes Booth: Edwin, you know there are thousands of people who agree with me. They'd love to see Lincoln in a grave.

Edwin Booth: There may be a lot of angry people out there, but I don't think anyone wants to see Lincoln dead.

Asia Booth: John, you have to remember that there are many people who support what Lincoln has done.

John Wilkes Booth: Not many that I know of. The abolition of slavery will destroy the South, as we know it. Just watch. I don't care what Lincoln says about Reconstruction—he's destroyed the country.

Edwin Booth: Let's change the subject and enjoy our dinner, John. We should simply agree to disagree on this matter.

Narrator 2: Booth cannot let his frustration rest. He meets with two boyhood friends, Samuel B. Arnold and Michael O'Laughlin, at Barnum's Hotel in Baltimore in late summer 1864.

John Wilkes Booth: Gentlemen, it's time we do something instead of just complaining about Lincoln.

Samuel B. Arnold: I agree, John. What do you have in mind?

John Wilkes Booth: A kidnapping.

Michael O'Laughlin: What purpose would that serve?

John Wilkes Booth: It's simple. We can demand that the Confederate prisoners be released in exchange for his return.

Samuel B. Arnold: How would we pull it off?

John Wilkes Booth: We'd just have to get enough men together to take him when he goes to the Soldiers' Home. Then we can get him to the Potomac and take him by boat to Richmond.

Michael O'Laughlin: The plan seems sound. It will be like being back in the army.

Samuel B. Arnold: You're right, Michael. Just another act of war . . .

John Wilkes Booth: Then if we're in agreement, I'll put the wheels in motion.

Narrator 1: Booth raises cash and purchases revolvers, handcuffs, and ammunition, which he delivers to Arnold and O'Laughlin in November. He delivers some stock and personal papers to Asia, telling her to open them if anything should happen to him.

Scene 3

Narrator 2: By the time of the inauguration on March 4, 1865, President Lincoln has angered even more people by refusing to accept peace unless the Confederates agree to all his terms—the Union and the abolition of slavery.

Narrator 1: One month later, Lincoln visits Richmond, Virginia, where the blacks treat him like a hero. Lincoln's enemies are infuriated, especially Booth. He listens to Lincoln speak on Reconstruction with two friends, Lewis Payne and David Herold.

John Wilkes Booth: I despise that man. Lewis, you have your gun, don't you?

Lewis Payne: Yes, why?

John Wilkes Booth: Shoot him! Shoot him now!

Lewis Payne: Are you crazy? No!

John Wilkes Booth: Thanks to him, the blacks will be citizens before long.

Lewis Payne: Come on, John. Let's get out of here.

John Wilkes Booth: That's the last speech he will ever make.

Lewis Payne: John, all you do is talk.

John Wilkes Booth: No, it's not all talk. You'll see.

Narrator 2: Booth has, in fact, been laying groundwork for taking action against Lincoln. Dr. Samuel A. Mudd helps Booth buy a horse and introduces him to John Harrison Surratt and Surratt's mother, Mary E. Surratt. Booth visits their tavern to talk with them about his frustration with President Lincoln. He discusses kidnapping plots with other sympathizers, including George Atzerodt.

Narrator 1: On April 14, 1865, Booth learns that Lincoln will be in the presidential box that evening for a performance of *Our American Cousin*. Booth arranges to meet Atzerodt, Payne, and Herold at a hotel near the theater at eight o'clock.

John Wilkes Booth: I'm going to take care of Lincoln at the play. Lewis, I want you to go to Seward's home and kill him. George, you take care of the vice president.

Narrator 2: Shortly after ten o'clock, Booth enters the presidential box, shoots President Lincoln, and leaps out of the box, breaking his ankle as he drops down on the stage. He hobbles out a rear door, climbs upon a waiting horse, and flees into the night.

Narrator 1: Meanwhile, Lewis Payne enters the home of Secretary of State William H. Seward, attacking him with a knife. Atzerodt does not try to kill Johnson.

Scene 4

Narrator 2: At 7:22 A.M. on April 15, President Lincoln is pronounced dead. Two days later, Mary Surratt, Lewis Payne, Sam Arnold, and Michael O'Laughlin are taken into custody.

Narrator 1: On April 26, Booth and Herold are surrounded in a barn on a farm near Port Royal, Virginia. Herold surrenders, and Booth dies from a gunshot wound while resisting arrest.

Narrator 2: On May 10, a military commission begins a trial of eight conspirators: Samuel B. Arnold, Michael O'Laughlin, David Herold, George Atzerodt, Lewis Payne, Mary Surratt, Dr. Samuel A. Mudd, and Edward Spangler, a stagehand at the Ford Theatre.

Narrator 1: The prosecution begins by establishing the circumstances surrounding the assassination of President Lincoln. James P. Ferguson, who owns a nearby restaurant, testifies.

James P. Ferguson: I saw John Wilkes Booth on the afternoon of the fourteenth between two and four o'clock, standing by the side of his horse. Mr. Maddox was standing by him talking.

Prosecuting Attorney: Were you at the performance?

James P. Ferguson: Yes. About one o'clock Mr. Harry Ford came into my place and said that General Grant was to be at the theater. I secured a seat directly opposite the President's box. I saw the President and his family when they came in.

Prosecuting Attorney: Did you see Mr. Booth that evening?

James P. Ferguson: Some time near ten o'clock I saw Booth pass near the President's box, and then stop and lean against the wall. After standing there a moment, I saw him step down one step, put his hands on the door and his knee against it, and push the door open—the first door that goes into the box.

Prosecuting Attorney: Then what happened?

James P. Ferguson: At that moment the President was shot. He was leaning his hand on the railing, looking down at a person in the orchestra. I saw the flash of the pistol right back in the box. As the person jumped over and landed on the stage I could see it was

Booth. He rose and exclaimed, *"Sic semper tyrannis,"* and ran directly across the stage to the opposite door, where the actors come in.

Prosecuting Attorney: What did you do?

James P. Ferguson: I saw that the President was hurt. I left the theater and went to the police station on D Street. I then ran up D Street to the house of Mr. Peterson, where the President was taken.

Narrator 2: Joseph Burroughs, an employee at the theater, is questioned about that night.

Joseph Burroughs: I carry bills for Ford's Theatre during the daytime and stand at the stage door at night. I knew John Wilkes Booth and used to attend to his horse. On the afternoon of the fourteenth of April he brought his horse to the stable between five and six o'clock. Between nine and ten o'clock Edward Spangler asked me to hold a horse. I held him as I sat on a bench by the house near there.

Prosecuting Attorney: Did you hear anything unusual?

Joseph Burroughs: I heard the report of the pistol. I got off the bench when Booth came out. He told me to give him his horse. He struck me with the butt of a knife and knocked me down. He did this as he was mounting his horse, with one foot in the stirrup. He also kicked me, and then rode off immediately.

Narrator 1: Next, the prosecution questions John M. Lloyd about the weapons secured by the Surratts.

John M. Lloyd: I reside at Mrs. Surratt's tavern, working in the hotel and doing farming. Some five or six weeks before the assassination of the President, John H. Surratt, David E. Herold, and George Atzerodt came to my house. They came into the bar and drank. Then John Surratt called me into the front parlor. On the sofa were two carbines, with ammunition, also a rope from sixteen to twenty feet in length, and a monkey wrench. Surratt asked me to take care of these things, and to conceal the carbines. I told them I did not wish to keep such things.

Prosecuting Attorney: Did you indeed hide them?

John M. Lloyd: Mr. Surratt took me to a room above the storeroom. He showed me where I could put them underneath the joists of the second floor on the main building. I put them in there according to his directions.

Prosecuting Attorney: What happened to the weapons?

John M. Lloyd: On the fourteenth of April Mrs. Surratt told me to have the shooting-irons ready by that evening. She told me to have two bottles of whiskey ready too. At about midnight Herold came for the things. Booth remained on his horse. They took only one of the carbines. Booth said he could not take his because his leg was broken.

Prosecuting Attorney: Did Herold say anything else to you?

John M. Lloyd: He said, "I will tell you some news. I am pretty certain we have assassinated the President and Secretary Seward."

Scene 5

Narrator 2: The prosecution next questions Louis J. Weichman, a boarder at the Surratts', about the allegations that Mr. Booth met regularly with the Surratts.

Louis J. Weichmann: On the second of April, Mrs. Surratt asked me to tell John Wilkes Booth that she wished to see him on private business. I conveyed the message, and Booth said he would come to the house in the evening as soon as he could.

Prosecuting Attorney: Did he come to the house?

Louis J. Weichmann: He did.

Prosecuting Attorney: Did you see Booth with Mrs. Surratt again?

Louis J. Weichmann: On the Tuesday previous to the assassination, I drove Mrs. Surratt to Surrattsville. We stopped at the house of Mr. Lloyd, who keeps a tavern there. I saw Mr. Booth speaking with Mrs. Surratt in the parlor. They were alone. Immediately after he left, Mrs. Surratt and I started back.

Prosecuting Attorney: Did you ever see Booth in conversation with Mr. Surratt?

Louis J. Weichmann: Booth frequently called at the Surratt's, asking for Mr. Surratt, and in his absence for Mrs. Surratt. Their interviews were always far apart from other persons. Sometimes they would go upstairs to speak in private, sometimes for two or three hours.

Defense Attorney: Did Mr. Surratt ever discuss a conspiracy to assassinate the President?

Louis J. Weichmann: He never intimated to me, nor to anyone else to my knowledge, that there was a plan to assassinate the President.

Defense Attorney: Were you ever asked to leave when Booth was conversing with Mr. Surratt?

Louis J. Weichmann: I cannot say that any objection was ever made by either of them. Their conversations, in my presence, were on general topics.

Narrator 1: The prosecution calls R. C. Morgan, who works for the War Department, to describe what happened at the Surrats' after the assassination.

Prosecuting Attorney: Describe what happened on the night of April seventeenth.

R. C. Morgan: Colonel Olcott, special commisioner of the War Department, sent me to the house of Mrs. Surratt to seize papers and arrest inmates of the house. While I was there, Lewis Payne came in with a pickax over his shoulder. He said he wanted to see Mrs. Surratt. I asked him why he had come and he said to dig a gutter for Mrs. Surratt. I asked him when and he said in the morning and that he had come to find out what time to come to work in the morning.

Prosecuting Attorney: Where was he from?

R. C. Morgan: He said he was from Virginia and that he preferred working with his pickax to serving in the army. I told him he'd have to go to the Provost Marshal's office and explain his business with Mrs. Surratt. He was taken and searched.

Prosecuting Attorney: What happened during the search?

R. C. Morgan: I found a photograph of John Wilkes Booth and a card that said *Sic Semper Tyrannis*. I also found a bullet-mold and some percussion caps in a room that I believe was Mrs. Surratt's room.

Narrator 2: The defense calls J. Z. Jenkins, an acquaintance of Mrs. Surrat's who testifies on her behalf.

Defense Attorney: Tell us about your knowledge of Mrs. Surratt and a possible conspiracy to assassinate President Lincoln.

J. Z. Jenkins: Mrs. Surratt has never, to my knowledge, breathed a word that was disloyal to the government. Nor have I ever heard her make any remark showing her to have knowledge of any plan or conspiracy to capture or assassinate the President or any member of the government. I have known her frequently to give milk, tea, and such refreshments as she had in her house to Union troops when they were passing.

Scene 6

Narrator 2: Jacob Ritterspaugh is questioned about Edward Spangler, the stagehand at the theater.

Jacob Ritterspaugh: I know the prisoner, Edward Spangler. He took his meals where I boarded, but he slept at the theater.

Prosecuting Attorney: What happened on the night of April fourteenth?

Jacob Ritterspaugh: I was standing on the stage behind the scenes when someone called out that the President was shot. I saw a man with no hat on running toward the back door. He had a knife in his hand, and I ran to stop him. He struck at me with the knife and I jumped back. He then ran out and slammed the door shut. By the time I opened the door, the man had got on his horse and was racing down the alley. I came back on the stage where I had left Edward Spangler.

Prosecuting Attorney: Did Spangler say anything to you?

Jacob Ritterspaugh: Spangler hit me on the face with the back of his hand and said, "Don't say which way he went." I asked him what he meant by slapping me in the mouth, and he said, "For God's sake, shut up."

Narrator 1: The prosecution establishes that George A. Atzerodt met with Booth at the home of John Greenawalt, who states that Atzerodt claimed he'd soon have enough gold to last him his lifetime. Another witness, Lieutenant W. R. Keim, testifies that Atzerodt regularly carried a knife and revolver.

Narrator 2: Mrs. Mary van Tine testifies that Booth often visited Michael O'Laughlin and Samuel Arnold at her boarding house. Various witnesses testify that Booth was often seen in the company of O'Laughlin and Arnold.

Narrator 1: William H. Bell, a servant in the home of Secretary of State William Seward, describes the events of the night of April fourteenth.

William H. Bell: I live at the house of Mr. Seward and attend to the door. That man, Lewis Payne, came to the door on the night of April fourteenth. He said he had medicine for Mr. Seward in a little package in his hand. He said he must go up, he must see him. He talked very rough to me. I told him he could not see Mr. Seward and that I would take the medicine up. He insisted, so I went up ahead of him. Mr. Frederick Seward, his son, said, "You cannot see him."

Prosecuting Attorney: What happened next?

William H. Bell: Payne started to come down. Then he jumped up and struck Mr. Frederick. Frederick fell back into his sister's room. Then I ran down the stairs to the front door, hollering "Murder." I got some soldiers and then saw that Payne was getting on a horse. I ran after him, but he got away.

Narrator 2: Sergeant George F. Robinson testifies about the attack on Secretary of State Seward.

Sergeant George F. Robinson: I was acting as an attendant to Mr. Seward, who was confined to his bed with injuries from being thrown from his carriage. I heard a disturbance in the hall and opened the door to see what the trouble was. That man, Lewis Payne, struck me with a knife in the forehead, knocked me partially down. He then struck Mr. Seward, wounding him. I tried to haul him off Mr. Seward's bed, and then he turned on me. I saw him strike Mr. Seward with the same knife with which he cut my forehead. Someone came in the room and grabbed him. Payne pulled away and ran downstairs.

Narrator 1: Colonel Henry H. Wells testifies regarding Dr. Samuel A. Mudd's role in treating Booth.

Colonel Henry H. Wells: During the week subsequent to the assassination, I had three interviews with Dr. Samuel A. Mudd. He said that at about four o'clock in the morning on the fifteenth of April, he was aroused by a loud knock at his door. A person held two horses, with another man with a broken leg sitting on his horse. Dr. Mudd helped the man into his house and examined the leg. Dr. Mudd said he dressed the limb as best he could and had his servant make a crutch for him.

Prosecuting Attorney: Did the injured man leave?

Colonel Henry H. Wells: I think he said the two persons remained until some time after dinner. He admitted that he recognized the person he treated as Booth. He said that the other man, David E. Herold, asked the way to Dr. Wilmer's, saying he was a friend.

Scene 7

Narrator 2: On June 29, 1865, after approximately six weeks of testimony, the military commission begins its deliberations in secret. The next day they announce their findings. David Herold, Mary Surratt, Lewis Payne, and George Atzerodt are found guilty and sentenced to die. Dr. Samuel Mudd, Michael O' Laughlin, and Samuel Arnold are found guilty and given life terms. Edward Spangler is sentenced to a prison term of six years.

Narrator 1: On July 5, 1865, President Johnson approves the sentences and verdicts. Herold, Surratt, Payne, and Atzerodt are hanged two days later. Michael O'Laughlin dies in prison on September 23, 1867. Edward Spangler is released from prison in 1871 and dies four years later. Dr. Mudd dies on June 10, 1883. Samuel Arnold dies on September 21, 1906. John Surratt, who fled the country, is captured in Europe in 1867. He is tried and released and lives until 1916, offering his own theories of the conspiracy through public speeches.

Narrator 2: Now that you have heard excerpts from the trial of the Lincoln conspiracy, do you agree with the military commission that the defendants conspired to assassinate Abraham Lincoln? Should Dr. Mudd have refused to treat Booth or did he fulfill his duty as a physician? Should the investigation have ended with the death of John Wilkes Booth? After all, the killer had been found. Would the outcome have been different in a civilian or a criminal court instead of a military court? Finally, would the outcome have been different if the defendants faced a jury today?

2
A Woman's Right

The United States vs.
Susan B. Anthony

Susan B. Anthony, women's rights advocate. AP Photo/New York University.

INTRODUCTION

Susan B. Anthony, an outspoken advocate of women's rights, along with thirteen other women, registered to vote in November 1872 in the state of New York. Reasoning that the Fourteenth Amendment applied to women, the inspectors at the registry allowed the women to cast their votes. Anthony was the only woman brought to trial, with the trial held at Canandaigua, New York, in June 1873. Miss Anthony's defense rested on her belief that she was legally entitled to vote and that if she wasn't legally entitled to vote, she voted in good faith in the belief that it was her right. Although this script is constructed so that the audience can act as the jury, the judge makes clear that the jury must bring a verdict of guilty. Use this script to explore the changes in attitudes toward rights of the accused, as well as those regarding the rights of women.

PRESENTATION SUGGESTIONS

Reflecting the attitudes toward women of the time period, Miss Anthony was not allowed to testify in her own behalf. Therefore, her only spoken part is during the sentencing portion of the trial. Except for the narrator, all other roles are male. (Beverly Jones, one of the inspectors, is a male.) Another limitation when presenting the trial is the lengthy defense presented by her attorney Harry Selden, who was also a witness in the case. Selden's defense is abbreviated here and presented in a series of short scenes. To provide more variety, consider having different readers, male and female, read Selden's part with each new scene. If this is performed for an audience, have the narrator explain that Selden's part is read by multiple readers. All players can remain on stage for the script.

RELATED BOOKS

Kendall, Martha E. *Susan B. Anthony: Voice for Women's Voting Rights.* Berkeley Heights, NJ: Enslow Publishing, 1997.

Monroe, Judy. *The Susan B. Anthony Women's Voting Rights Trial: A Headline Court Case.* Berkeley Heights, NJ: Enslow Publishing, 2002.

CHARACTERS

Narrator

Richard Crowley, *prosecuting attorney*

Beverly W. Jones, *elections inspector*

Harry Selden (optional multiple readers), *defense attorney*

Ward Hunt, *judge*

Clerk of the Court

Susan B. Anthony, *women's rights advocate*

A Woman's Right

The United States vs. Susan B. Anthony

Scene 1

Narrator: The trial of Susan B. Anthony begins in June 1873 in the state of New York. The jury faces a decision about whether women had the right to vote. Attorney Richard Crowley opens the trial with a description of the charges against Miss Anthony.

Richard Crowley: On the fifth of November, 1872, there was held in this state a general election for candidates to the Congress of the United States. The defendant, Miss Susan B. Anthony, at the time resided in the city of Rochester, New York, and upon the fifth day of November, 1872, she voted for a representative in the United States Congress and also for a representative for the State of New York. At that time she was a woman. I suppose there will be no question about that. The question is whether my client here had done anything to justify her being consigned to a felon's prison. I shall endeavor to establish that when she registered and voted, she was as much entitled to vote as any man that voted.

    Before the registration and before this election, Miss Anthony called upon me for advice upon the question whether, under the Fourteenth Amendment of the Constitution of the United States, she had a right vote. After examination of the law, I advised her that she was as lawful a voter as I am, and I advised her to go and offer her vote. I believe she acted in good faith, according to her right as the law and Constitution gave it to her. If she made a mistake, or if I made one, that is not a reason for committing her to a felon's cell.

Narrator: Mr. Crowley begins the government's case by calling Beverly W. Jones to testify.

Richard Crowley: Do you know the defendant, Miss Susan B. Anthony?

Beverly W. Jones: Yes, sir.

Richard Crowley: In what capacity were you acting upon Election Day?

Beverly W. Jones: Inspector of election in the first district.

Richard Crowley: Upon the fifth day of November, did the defendant, Susan B. Anthony, vote in the first election district of the 8th ward of the city of Rochester?

Beverly W. Jones: Yes, sir.

Richard Crowley: Did you see her vote?

Beverly W. Jones: Yes, sir.

Richard Crowley: Did you receive the tickets from Miss Anthony?

Beverly W. Jones: Yes, sir.

Richard Crowley: What did you do with them when you received them?

Beverly W. Jones: Put them in the separate boxes where they belonged.

Richard Crowley: Was Miss Anthony challenged upon that occasion?

Beverly W. Jones: On that day she wasn't.

Narrator: Harry Selden cross-examines Mr. Jones next.

Harry Selden: Was there a registry of voters prior to the election?

Beverly W. Jones: Yes, sir.

Harry Selden: Were you one of the officers at the registration?

Beverly W. Jones: Yes, sir.

Harry Selden: Did Miss Anthony appear before the Board of Registry and claim to be registered as a voter?

Beverly W. Jones: She did.

Harry Selden: Was there any objection made as to her right to vote?

Beverly W. Jones: There was.

Harry Selden: On what grounds?

Beverly W. Jones: That the constitution of the State of New York did not allow women to vote.

Harry Selden: Did the board decide she was entitled to register?

Beverly W. Jones: Yes, sir.

Harry Selden: And she was registered accordingly?

Beverly W. Jones: Yes, sir.

Narrator: After a few follow-up questions by Mr. Crowley, the United States rests its case. Harry Selden offers himself as a witness for Susan B. Anthony, repeating his points in the opening statement that he had advised Anthony that she could legally register and vote. He is not cross-examined.

Harry Selden: I call Miss Anthony to respond to the question of the intention or belief under which she voted.

Richard Crowley: She is not competent as a witness in her own behalf.

Ward Hunt: The court agrees.

Narrator: Mr. Selden's case rests on Miss Anthony's testimony. Having been denied the opportunity to call Miss Anthony as a witness, he has no choice but to rest his case and hope that he can win by presenting compelling arguments on behalf of his client.

Scene 2

Narrator: Mr. Selden begins his arguments regarding the legal issues surrounding the case by quoting the law.

Harry Selden: The words of the Senate, so far as they are material in this case, are as follows: "If at any election for representative or delegate in the Congress of the United States, any person shall knowingly vote without having a lawful right to vote, every such person shall be deemed guilty of a crime, and on conviction thereof shall be punished by a fine not exceeding $500, or by imprisonment for a term not exceeding three years, or by both, in the discretion of the court, and shall pay the costs of prosecution."

The only alleged ground of illegality of the defendant's vote is that she is a woman. If the same act had been done by her brother under the same circumstances, the act would have been not only innocent, but also honorable and laudable. But having been done by a woman, it is said to be a crime. The crime consists not of the act, but of the simple fact that the person doing it was a woman. I believe this is the first instance in which a woman has been arraigned in a criminal court, merely on account of her sex.

Women have the same interest that men have in the establishment and maintenance of good government. Just like men, they are bound to obey the laws. They suffer to the same extent by bad laws, and profit to the same extent by good laws. It would seem that they should be allowed equally with men to express their preference in the choice of lawmakers and rulers.

I am aware, however, that we are governed by the Constitution and laws as they are, and that if the defendant has been guilty of violating the law, she must submit to the penalty, however unjust or absurd the law may be.

The principle argument against extending the vote to women is based upon the position that women are represented in the government by men, and that their rights and interests are better protected through that indirect representation than they would be by giving them a direct voice in the government.

I will share an example of the failings of such representation through a story. A young mother and her child came to live with the child's grandmother in Rochester, some time prior to 1860. The husband had abandoned the young family. Later, he returned from the west. He succeeded in getting the child into his custody and was taking the child to his home in the west, having somewhat clandestinely obtained possession of the child. The judge, following the traditional views of husband's rights, remanded the infant to the custody of the father. He thought the law required it, and perhaps it did. But if mothers had had a voice, either in making or in administering the law, I think the result would have been different. You can only imagine the distress of the mother on being thus separated from her child. The separation proved a final one—in less than a year neither father nor mother had any child to love or care for. The child had died. Whether the loss to the little one of a mother's love and watchfulness had any effect upon the result, cannot, of course, be known. . . .

Scene 3

Narrator: Selden continues his argument with a discussion of the changes of the law of the past twenty-five years.

Harry Selden: Prior to 1848, all the personal property of every woman became the absolute property of the husband upon marriage. He could squander it, and the wife could not touch or interfere with it. Prior to 1860, the husband could by will take the custody of his infant children away from the surviving mother, and give custody to whom he pleased—and he could in like manner dispose of the control of the children's property without the mother's consent. In most of these respects the state of the law has undergone great changes within the last twenty-five years. The property, real and personal, that a woman possesses before marriage, and such as may be given to her, remains her own, and is free from the control of her husband.

If a married woman is slandered, she can prosecute the slanderer in her own name and recover damages for the injury. The mother now has an equal claim with the father to the custody of their minor children, and courts may award the custody to either in their discretion. The husband cannot now appoint a guardian for his infant children without the consent of the mother, if living.

How have these changes been produced? Mainly as the result of the work of a few heroic women, one of whom stands arraigned as a criminal before this court today. For a thousand years, the absurdities and cruelties to which I have alluded have been embedded in common law and in the statute books. Men have not touched them and would not until the end of time, had they not been goaded to it by the persistent efforts of noble women like Miss Anthony.

Much has been done, but much more remains to be done. If women had been allowed to vote, the reforms that have taken twenty-five years would have been accomplished in a year. Women are still subject to taxation upon their property, without any voice as to the use of the tax. They are still subject to laws made by men. When brought to trial, no woman is allowed a place on the bench or in the jury box. They must suffer the penalty of such laws, made and administered solely by men, and be silent. Give them the ballot, and valuable reforms will be introduced that are not now thought of. Schools, almshouses, and hospitals will feel their influence. Women will not be taxed without an opportunity to be heard. They will not be subject to fines and imprisonment by laws made exclusively by men for doing what men have the right to do.

Scene 4

Narrator: Selden then broadens the scope of his argument to the treatment of women throughout the world.

Harry Selden: Let us look at the matter historically and on a broader field. If Chinese women were allowed an equal share with men in shaping the laws of that great empire, would they subject their female children to torture with bandaged feet in order that they might be cripples for the rest of their lives?

If Hindu women could have shaped the laws of India, would widows for ages have been burned on the funeral pyres of their deceased husbands?

If Jewish women had had a voice in framing Jewish laws, would the husband, at any time, have been allowed to divorce his wife and send her out of his house?

Would women in Turkey or Persia have made it a heinous, if not capital, offense for a wife to be seen abroad with her face not covered by an impenetrable veil?

Would women in England have been for ages subjected to execution for offenses for which men were given a few months imprisonment?

The principle that governs these cases is the same everywhere. Those who succeed in obtaining power, no matter by what means, will, with rare exceptions, use it for their exclusive benefit.

Scene 5

Narrator: Selden now reviews several amendments in his defense of Miss Anthony.

Harry Selden: The Thirteenth Amendment states that slavery is not allowed except as punishment for a crime. The Fourteenth Amendment provides that all persons born or naturalized in the United States are citizens. These citizens shall not be deprived of life, liberty, or property, without due process of law. Further, such citizens have the right to vote if they are male and twenty-one years of age. The Fifteenth Amendment states that citizens shall not be denied the right to vote based on race, color, or previous condition of servitude.

With the adoption of the Fourteenth Amendment, the United States has declared that all persons born or naturalized in the United States have the rights of citizenship. Therefore, I insist that the act of voting by Miss Anthony was lawful.

It has been said that the subject of allowing women to vote was not considered in the preparation or adoption of these amendments. That is immaterial. It is never possible to arrive at the intention of the people in adopting constitutions, except by referring to the language used.

Some say that women do not wish to vote. Certainly, many women do not, but that is no reason for denying the right to those who want to vote. Many men decline to vote. Is that a reason for denying the right to those who would vote?

Another objection is that the right to hold office goes with the right to vote, and that women are not qualified to discharge the duties of responsible offices. I can only ask one question: How many of the men who vote are qualified to hold office?

Let's look at the world again. In England, women have held many offices—those of constable, church warden, overseer of the poor, keeper of the "gate house" [a public prison], governess of a house of correction, sheriffs of counties, and high constable of England. How often have women, such as Queen Victoria, governed large kingdoms?

Another objection is that women cannot serve as soldiers. To this I answer that capacity for military service has never been made a test of the right to vote. If it were, young men from sixteen to twenty-one would be entitled to vote, and old men from sixty and upwards would not.

Therefore, on the constitutional grounds to which I have referred, Miss Anthony had a lawful right to vote. Her vote was properly received and counted. The first section of the Fourteenth Amendment secured that right and did not need the aid of any further legislation.

If Miss Anthony had dressed in men's apparel and assumed a man's name or resorted to any other artifice to deceive the board of inspectors, the jury might properly pronounce her guilty of the offense charged. All I claim is that she voted in perfect good faith, believing that it was her right, and has committed no crime.

I thank Your Honor for the great patience with which you have listened to my extended remarks.

Scene 6

Narrator: Judge Ward Hunt addresses the jury, having prepared his statement in writing.

Ward Hunt: The defendant is indicted under the act of Congress of 1870 for having voted for representatives of Congress in November 1872. This act makes it an offense for any person to vote without having a right to vote. The defendant is charged with not having a right to vote because she is a woman. The defendant insists that she has a right to vote, that the provision of the Constitution limiting the right to vote to persons of the male sex is in violation of the Fourteenth Amendment of the Constitution of the United States.

The Thirteenth, Fourteenth, and Fifteenth Amendments were designed mainly for the protection of the newly emancipated slaves. The Thirteenth Amendment provided that slavery should not exist in the United States. The Fourteenth Amendment created and defined citizenship of the United States. The Fifteenth Amendment guarantees the right to vote.

If the Fifteenth Amendment had contained the word "sex," the argument of the defendant would have been potent. However, the amendment is limited to race, color, or previous condition of servitude. The Legislature of the State of New York has seen fit to say that the voting shall be limited to the male sex. In saying this, there is, in my judgment, no violation of the letter or of the spirit of the Fourteenth or of the Fifteenth Amendment.

The Fourteenth Amendment gives no right to a woman to vote. If Miss Anthony believed she had a right to vote, does that relieve her from the penalty? Two principles apply here: First, ignorance of the law excuses no one; second, every person is presumed to understand and to intend the necessary effects of his own acts. Miss Anthony knew that she was a woman, and that the constitution of this state prohibits her from voting. She intended to violate that provision—intended to test it, perhaps, but certainly intended to violate it. She takes the risk, and she cannot escape the consequences.

Assuming that Miss Anthony believed she had a right to vote, that fact constitutes no defense if in truth she had not the right. She voluntarily voted illegally, and thus is subject to the penalty of the law. Upon this evidence I suppose there is no question for the jury and that the jury should find a verdict of guilty.

Narrator: Selden argues against the judge's instructions to the jury that they should find the defendant guilty.

Harry Selden: I ask Your Honor to submit to the jury these propositions: First, if the defendant, at the time of voting, believed that she had a right to vote and voted in good faith, she is not guilty. Second, in determining the question of whether she believed that she had a right to vote, the jury may take into consideration the advice that she received regarding the law. Third, that they may also take into consideration the fact that the inspectors considered the question and came to the conclusion that she had a right to vote. Fourth, that the jury has a right to find a general verdict of guilty or not guilty, as they shall believe that she has or has not committed the offense.

Narrator: And now, you the audience must weigh the facts as you have heard them. Judge Hunt has directed the jury to find a verdict of guilty. Mr. Selden has argued that the jury should be allowed to return a verdict of guilty or not guilty. If you were jury, would you want the right to choose a verdict? If you had the right to choose a verdict, how would you rule? How do you think the judge is going to respond to Mr. Seldon's request to let the jury choose their own verdict?

Scene 7

Narrator: Judge Hunt responds to Mr. Selden's request to let the jury choose their own verdict.

Ward Hunt: The question, gentlemen of the jury, is wholly a question of law. I have decided that under the Fourteenth Amendment Miss Anthony was not protected in a right to vote. And I have decided also that her belief and the advice that she took do not protect her. I therefore direct that you find a verdict of guilty.

Harry Selden: No court has the power to give that direction in a criminal case.

Ward Hunt: Take the verdict, Mr. Clerk.

Clerk: Gentlemen of the jury, hearken to your verdict of guilty as the court has recorded it.

Harry Selden: I certainly must except to the direction of the court that the jury should find a verdict of guilty. Will the clerk poll the jury?

Clerk: No. Gentlemen of the jury, you are discharged.

Scene 8

Narrator: The next day, Mr. Selden makes a motion for a new trial. After Judge Hunt denies the motion, the sentencing hearing proceeds.

Ward Hunt: Miss Anthony, please stand up. Has the prisoner anything to say why sentence shall not be pronounced?

Susan B. Anthony: Yes, Your Honor, I have many things to say; for in your ordered verdict of guilty, you have trampled every vital principle of our government. My rights are ignored. Robbed of the fundamental privilege of citizenship, I am degraded from the status of a citizen to that of a subject. All of my sex are, by Your Honor's verdict, doomed to political subjection under this so-called form of government.

Ward Hunt: The court cannot listen to a rehearsal of arguments the prisoner's counsel has already consumed three hours in presenting.

Susan B. Anthony: May it please Your Honor, I am not arguing the question, but simply stating the reasons why a sentence cannot, in justice, be pronounced against me. I have been denied the right to a trial by a jury of my peers and therefore denied my sacred rights to life, liberty, property, and—

Ward Hunt: The court cannot allow the prisoner to go on.

Susan B. Anthony: But Your Honor will not deny me this one and only poor privilege of protest against this high-handed outrage upon my citizen's rights. May it please the court to remember that since the day of my arrest last November, this is the first time that either myself or any person of my disfranchised class has been allowed a word of defense before judge or jury—

Ward Hunt: The prisoner must sit down. The court cannot allow it.

Susan B. Anthony: All of my prosecutors, from the eighth ward corner grocery politician who entered the complaint, to the United States Marshal, Commissioner, District Attorney, District Judge, Your Honor on the bench—not one is my peer, but each and all are my political sovereigns. Had Your Honor submitted my case to the jury, as was clearly your duty, even then I should have had just cause of protest, for not one of those men was my peer.

Ward Hunt: The prisoner has been tried according to the established forms of law.

Susan B. Anthony: Yes, Your Honor, but by forms of law all made by men, interpreted by men, administered by men, in favor of men, and against women; and hence, your honor's ordered verdict of guilty; against a United States citizen for the exercise of "that citizen's right to vote," simply because that citizen was a woman and not a man. But, yesterday, the same man-made forms of law, declared it a crime punishable with $1,000 fine and six months imprisonment, for you, or me, or both of us, to give a cup of cold water, a crust of bread, or a night's shelter to a panting fugitive as he was tracking his way to Canada. And every man or woman in whose veins coursed a drop of human sympathy violated that wicked law, reckless of consequences, and was justified in so doing. Just as the slaves fought for freedom, so now must women take their right to a voice in this government. I have taken mine, and mean to take it at every possible opportunity.

Ward Hunt: The court orders the prisoner to sit down. It will not allow another word.

Susan B. Anthony: When I was brought before Your Honor for trial, I hoped for a broad and liberal interpretation of the Constitution and its recent amendments that should declare all United States citizens to have equal rights. Failing to get this justice, failing even to get a trial by a jury of my peers, I ask not leniency at your hands, but rather the full rigors of the law.

Judge Hunt: The court must insist—

Narrator: Miss Anthony sits down.

Judge Hunt: The prisoner will stand up.

Narrator: Miss Anthony stands up again.

Ward Hunt: The sentence of the court is that you pay a fine of one hundred dollars and the costs of the prosecution.

Susan B. Anthony: May it please Your Honor; I shall never pay a dollar of your unjust penalty. All the stock in trade I possess is a $10,000 debt, incurred by publishing my paper, *The Revolution,* four years ago. The sole object of my paper was to educate all women to do precisely as I have done, rebel against your man-made, unjust, unconstitutional forms of law, that tax, fine, imprison, and hang women, while they deny them the right of representation in the government. I shall work to pay every dollar of that honest debt, but not a penny shall go to this unjust claim. And I shall earnestly and persistently continue to urge all women to the practical recognition of the old revolutionary maxim, that "Resistance to tyranny is obedience to God."

Narrator: Miss Anthony petitions Congress on January 12, 1874, to have the fine remitted. Congress does not act on the petition. Anthony never pays her fine and she does not live to see women given the right to vote. The Nineteenth Amendment, which grants women the right to vote, is introduced in 1878. Suffragettes work tirelessly for this important right until it is ratified on August 18, 1920.

3

She Took an Axe . . .

The Commonwealth of Massachusetts vs. Lizzie Borden

Lizzie Borden, defendant in the murder of Abby and Andrew Borden. AP Photo/fls.

INTRODUCTION

Lizzie Borden took an axe
And gave her mother forty whacks.
And when she saw what she had done,
She gave her father forty-one.

The nation was shocked when news broke that Andrew Borden and his second wife, Abby, were brutally killed with a hatchet on a hot August day in 1892 in Fall River, Massachusetts. The case became scandalous when Lizzie, Andrew's daughter and Abby's stepdaughter, was accused of killing the couple. A woman of her upbringing could not possibly be a murderer, could she? The trial was carefully followed, and many books subsequently have been written with various theories about whether Lizzie actually killed her father and stepmother. The above rhyme, immortalizing Lizzie's presumed guilt, contains several errors. The killer used a hatchet, not an ax, and Abby received eighteen blows, while Andrew received eleven blows. After reading the trial, the students may want to explore alternate theories about the truth behind the murders.

PRESENTATION SUGGESTIONS

Have the characters stand in the following order: narrators, William Moody, Hosea Knowlton, Alice Russell, Dr. Bowen, Abby Borden, Andrew Borden, Emma Borden (seated), Lizzie Borden (seated), Bridget Sullivan, Adelaide Churchill, Thomas Kieran, Andrew Jennings, Melvin O. Adams, George D. Robinson. Josiah Blaisdell, Justin Dewey, and the foreman should stand behind Emma and Lizzie Borden. Abby and Andrew Borden can sit after Scene 3. Characters can be dressed in clothing appropriate to their roles of the late 1800s, such as dark dresses for the women, suits for the men, modest clothing for the neighbors.

RELATED BOOKS

Rappaport, Doreen. *The Lizzie Borden Trial.* New York: HarperCollins, 1992. Grades 4–7.
Rebello, Leonard. *Lizzie Borden Past and Present.* Fall River, MA: Al-Zach Press, 1999. Comprehensive reference book.
Schuetz, Janice. *The Logic of Women on Trial: Case Studies of Popular American Trials.* Carbondale, IL: Southern Illinois University Press, 1994.
Spierling, Frank. *Lizzie.* New York: Random House, 1984.

THE COMMONWEALTH OF MASSACHUSETTS VS. LIZZIE BORDEN

CHARACTERS

Narrator 1

Narrator 2

Emma Borden, *sister to Lizzie Borden*

Lizzie Borden, *the accused*

Abby Borden, *stepmother of Emma and Lizzie Borden*

Andrew Borden, *father of Emma and Lizzie Borden*

Alice Russell, *neighbor to the Bordens*

Bridget Sullivan, *servant to the Bordens*

Adelaide Churchill, *neighbor to the Bordens*

Dr. Bowen

William Moody, *prosecuting attorney*

Andrew Jennings, *defense attorney*

Thomas Kieran, *investigating officer*

Hosea Knowlton, *prosecuting attorney*

Melvin O. Adams, *defense attorney*

George D. Robinson, *defense attorney*

Josiah Blaisdell, *presiding judge*

Justin Dewey, *associate justice*

Foreman

She Took an Axe . . .

The Commonwealth of Massachusetts vs. Lizzie Borden

Scene 1

Narrator 1: Mr. Andrew Borden, age seventy, is a prosperous man. He owns considerable commercial properties and serves on several boards of directors. In 1892, the community of Fall River, Massachusetts, respects a man such as Andrew Borden.

Narrator 2: In spite of his wealth, Mr. Borden finds it difficult to shed the thrifty habits that helped him build his wealth. His home is modest. The only water sources inside the house are cold-water taps in the kitchen and in the basement laundry room. The single toilet is also in the basement.

Narrator 1: Emma, age forty-one, and Lizzie, age thirty-two, still live with their father and stepmother, Abby. Although Abby and Andrew Borden have been married since Lizzie was five, both Emma and Lizzie resent this substitute for their deceased mother. For years Lizzie, who is very close to her sister, has addressed their stepmother as "Mrs. Borden."

Emma Borden: Lizzie, supper is ready. Are you going to eat anything?

Lizzie Borden: I'm going to eat, but not with "them." I'm still upset with Father.

Emma Borden: I'll have Maggie bring you a tray then.

Lizzie Borden: Have Maggie bring supper for both of us. We have to talk about something.

Emma Borden: All right. I'll be back shortly.

Narrator 2: Maggie, in her mid-twenties, whose name is actually Bridget Sullivan, cleans and cooks for the Bordens. A previous housekeeper was named Maggie and the sisters never broke the habit of using the name Maggie instead of Bridget.

Narrator 1: Over supper, Lizzie wastes no time in getting to the point.

Lizzie Borden: Emma, I just can't get over what Father has done. How could he give the farm to *her* family?

Emma Borden: I don't understand it either. That farm should go to us, not our stepmother's relatives. Just think of the summers we spent there.

Lizzie Borden: I think it's only going to get worse. And I know Uncle John has been behind a lot of this.

Emma Borden: I don't understand that either. He is our mother's brother! You'd think he'd have our interests at heart instead of our stepmother's. If father dies first and she gets everything, we'll end up with nothing. She'll make sure everything goes to her family. We'll be poor and they'll be rich.

Lizzie Borden: If only Mother hadn't died. You know, I can't even remember her.

Emma Borden: You were so young, Lizzie. I've tried to take care of you. I just wish *she* had never shown up.

Lizzie Borden: Well, she did. Now, what are we going to do about all this? It's so infuriating.

Emma Borden: Well, I'm going to get away, Lizzie. I can't stand to be in this house with them. I'm going to visit Jennie Brownell for a few days. Why don't you come along and visit your friends in Marion? Maybe if we have some time away we can think this through. There has to be a way to make Father see that he's being terribly unfair.

Lizzie Borden: I don't know if Father will ever listen to reason, especially with Uncle John and Mrs. Borden working against us. But perhaps getting away will help for a while.

Narrator 2: On a steamy July day in 1892, Emma and Lizzie travel together on part of their journey. Lizzie decides to turn back while Emma continues to Fairhaven. First, Lizzie checks into a boarding house. Then she returns in despair to her home at 92 Second Street.

Scene 2

Narrator 1: On August 1, Andrew and Abby Borden sit down to a dinner of mutton and vegetables, prepared by Bridget.

Abby Borden: Andrew, is Lizzie joining us for dinner?

Andrew Borden: No, she said she's not hungry.

Abby Borden: She seems so angry.

Andrew Borden: She'll calm down. She's still upset over the farm.

Abby Borden: I think it's more than that.

Andrew Borden: *(abruptly)* Let's just enjoy our dinner, all right? This mutton is delicious.

Narrator 2: That afternoon, Abby begins to feel ill. Her throat hurts and her stomach has become queasy. By three o'clock in the morning she has terrible cramps. Thinking that water will help, she goes downstairs to the water faucet. After drinking the water, she begins to vomit. Andrew finds her lying on the kitchen floor when he gets up the next morning.

Narrator 1: Mrs. Borden continues to feel ill throughout the day. That evening Andrew wakes her.

Abby Borden: *(weakly)* I've been poisoned! I've got to see Dr. Bowen!

Andrew Borden: Nonsense! You've probably just eaten something disagreeable. Don't bother him with this.

Abby Borden: I have been *poisoned,* I tell you.

Andrew Borden: Come now. Just go to sleep. You'll be fine in the morning.

Narrator 2: The next morning, Abby, still feeling sick, notices red splotches on her arms and legs. She dresses and staggers toward the front door. Dr. Seabury Bowen lives across the street. Andrew sees her moving toward the front door.

Andrew Borden: Where are you going?!

Abby Borden: I have to see the doctor!

Andrew Borden: I won't pay for it!

Narrator 1: Abby leaves to see the doctor, who listens to Abby's story and then crosses the street to ask Andrew about Abby's illness. Andrew angrily sends him away. By afternoon, Andrew has begun to feel ill as well, but he ignores his nausea and meets with John Morse, who has returned to discuss the terms of Andrew's will.

Narrator 2: Later, Lizzie pays a call on Alice Russell, a neighbor and close friend of Emma.

Lizzie Borden: Alice, I need to confide in someone.

Alice Russell: What is the trouble, Lizzie?

Lizzie Borden: I feel so depressed. It's as if something's hanging over me.

Alice Russell: What do you think it is?

Lizzie Borden: I don't know. Father has so much trouble. And last night he and Abby were violently ill.

Alice Russell: Was it something they'd eaten?

Lizzie Borden: I don't know. We were all sick, all but Maggie.

Alice Russell: What did you eat?

Lizzie Borden: We had some bread from the bakery. Everyone ate some but Maggie.

Alice Russell: Well, it couldn't have been the bread or others would have gotten sick.

Lizzie Borden: Maybe our milk was poisoned.

Alice Russell: But how could someone tamper with the milk?

Lizzie Borden: I don't know. It's just that Father and Abby were so sick. Sometimes I feel afraid that Father has an enemy. He has so much trouble with men who come to see him. Father had a terrible argument with a man over some property. Father ordered him out of the house. Someone broke into the barn—and even into the house, in broad daylight, with Emma and Maggie and me there.

Alice Russell: I've never heard of that before.

Lizzie Borden: Father doesn't want us to talk of it. Father wouldn't even let Abby go to see Dr. Bowen this morning. She thought she'd been poisoned, but Father said he wouldn't pay for her to go. She went anyway. Then Father was so rude to Dr. Bowen—I was mortified. I don't know what we're going to do.

Scene 3

Narrator 1: There are five people in the Borden house on the morning of August 4, 1892. Abby is gradually recovering, while Andrew continues to ignore his nausea and weakness. Bridget awakens, violently ill. While Bridget struggles with her morning chores, Abby instructs her on the breakfast menu. John Morse dresses and joins Andrew and Abby for a large breakfast at seven o'clock. After John Morse leaves to visit other family members, Lizzie comes downstairs.

Lizzie Borden: Has Uncle John left?

Abby: Yes, he'll be back at noon for dinner.

Lizzie Borden: I'm sorry I missed him.

Narrator 2: Andrew leaves for work. Bridget suddenly leaves the room and vomits in the backyard. When she returns, she looks pale and weak.

Abby: Bridget, it's almost 9:30. Don't forget that you are to wash the windows today.

Bridget Sullivan: *(weakly)* Yes, Ma'am.

Abby: I'm going to tidy up John's room. Don't waste any more time.

Bridget Sullivan: Yes, Ma'am.

Narrator 1: Bridget laboriously hauls water and washes the main floor outside windows. By mid-morning she has moved inside the house. She hears a noise at the front door and unlocks it, letting in Andrew, who brings in the mail and goes into the dining room.

Lizzie Borden: How are you feeling?

Andrew: No better, no worse.

Lizzie Borden: Is there any mail for me?

Andrew: None. How is Abby?

Lizzie Borden: She received a note from someone and went out.

Narrator 2: Andrew lies down on the sitting room couch, while Lizzie goes into the dining room to chat with Bridget, who is cleaning the inside windows.

Lizzie Borden: Are you going out this afternoon?

Bridget Sullivan: I don't know. I don't feel all that well.

Lizzie Borden: Mrs. Borden has gone out on a sick call. I might go out too.

Bridget Sullivan: Who is sick?

Lizzie Borden: I don't know. She got a note his morning. *(she pauses briefly)* You know, there's a sale of dress goods at Sargent's this afternoon.

Bridget Sullivan: I'm going to go there then!

Narrator 1: Taking advantage of Mrs. Borden's absence, Bridget goes to her room to rest before lunch and her planned afternoon shopping trip.

Scene 4

Narrator 2: At 11:10, Lizzie's voice disrupts the quiet of the house.

Lizzie Borden: Maggie! Come down!

Bridget Sullivan: What's the matter?

Lizzie Borden: Come down quick! Father's dead! Somebody killed him!

Narrator 1: Bridget comes down and starts to go into the sitting room.

Lizzie Borden: Don't go in there! It's awful! Run over and get the doctor!

Narrator 2: The doctor is out but his wife sends for him. Lizzie sends Bridget to neighbor Alice Russell's. Meanwhile, Adelaide Churchill, who lives in the next house over, returns from purchasing groceries. She sees Lizzie at the door, looking distressed.

Adelaide Churchill: Lizzie, what is the matter?

Lizzie Borden: Oh, Mrs. Churchill, please come over. Someone has killed Father!

Adelaide Churchill: Where is he, Lizzie?

Lizzie Borden: In the sitting room.

Narrator 1: Mrs. Churchill looks in the sitting room and gasps.

Adelaide Churchill: Where were you when it happened?

Lizzie Borden: I was in the barn . . . I went to get some iron.

Adelaide Churchill: Where is your mother?

Lizzie Borden: I don't know. She got a note to go see someone who is sick. We've all been very sick. We think we've been poisoned. Dr. Bowen isn't home. I must have a doctor.

Adelaide Churchill: I'll try to get one.

Narrator 2: Mrs. Churchill sends her handyman for a doctor. When she returns, she finds Bridget there and Dr. Bowen is just arriving.

Dr. Bowen: Have you seen anybody around the place, Lizzie?

Lizzie Borden: I have not.

Dr. Bowen: *(to Mrs. Churchill)* Bring a sheet to cover him.

Lizzie Borden: Dr. Bowen, would you send a telegram to Emma?

Dr. Bowen: Of course, I'll be right back.

Lizzie Borden: *(to Bridget)* Could you look for Mrs. Borden? I thought I heard her come in.

Narrator 1: Mrs. Churchill and Bridget explore the house together while Alice Russell stays with Lizzie. They see part of Mrs. Borden's body and they return downstairs, distraught.

Adelaide Churchill: There's another one.

Lizzie Borden: I have to get over to Oak Grove Cemetery to see about things.

Adelaide Churchill: Oh, no. The undertaker will see to everything. . . .

Narrator 2: By the time Dr. Bowen returns from sending the telegram, the police have arrived. Officer Michael Mullaly asks Lizzie if there are any hatchets or axes in the house. She responds that there are several, and she asks Bridget to take him to the cellar where he discovers several axes.

Narrator 1: Upstairs, Officer Wixon notes that Abby's blood has coagulated, while Andrew's blood is running freely. He concludes that more than an hour had passed between the killings. By three o'clock, the police allow the medical examiner, Dr. William A. Dolan, to conduct autopsies of the bodies on the dining room table.

Narrator 2: Emma returns early in the evening. By this time Lizzie has endured endless questions.

Narrator 1: By August 11, Judge Blaisdell has concluded an inquest. Lizzie is indicted, and a grand jury investigation begins on November 7th. The evidence is sparse, and it appears that there will not be a trial. Then Alice Russell testifies that she observed Lizzie burning a dress in the kitchen stove three days after the murders. Lizzie Borden is subsequently charged with three counts of murder: that of her father, her stepmother, and the murders of both of them. The trial is set for June 5, 1893.

Scene 5

Narrator 2: The press gathers in New Bedford, the county seat, for the scandalous trial of Lizzie Borden. Chief Justice Albert Mason is joined by Associate Justices Caleb Blodgett and Justin Dewey for the trial. Twelve jurors, all male, have been chosen from more than one hundred potential jurors.

Narrator 1: William H. Moody, District Attorney of Essex County, begins the prosecution's case.

William Moody: Upon the fourth day of August of last year, an old man and woman, without a known enemy, in their own home, in the light of day, were both killed, one after the other. Today, a woman of good social position, a member of the church, active in good works, and the daughter of one of the victims, is accused of these crimes.

Narrator 2: Moody describes the events of the morning, emphasizing Andrew's wealth and how Lizzie hated Abby.

William Moody: There was so much blood spattered that it would be probable that blood would be on the person or the clothing of the assailant. No blood was found on the dress the defendant is said to have worn that morning. However, Alice Russell will tell you that the defendant wore a different dress when she arrived that morning. She will also tell you that the defendant burned another dress because she claimed it was covered with paint.

Narrator 1: Moody holds up the hatchet with the missing handle, describing how it was covered with a coarse dust of ashes. He tells the jury that an officer noticed something the shape of a large roll of paper burning in the stove, insisting that it was the hatchet's missing handle.

Narrator 2: Moody also asserts that Lizzie must have lied when she claimed she hadn't seen her stepmother's body when coming up the stairs.

William Moody: We shall prove that this prisoner has made contradictory statements about her whereabouts that morning. Then we shall ask you whether any other explanation can be given for the sad events that happened upon the morning of August 4th.

Narrator 1: Moody's key points will be the burning of the dress, the hatchet, and Lizzie's claim to be in the barn finding iron for a fishing sinker. Moody calls Thomas Kieran, a professional engineer called in to prepare a detailed map of the crime scene and neighborhood. His testimony is expected to be routine. Then Andrew Jennings, the Borden family lawyer, cross-examines Kieran.

Andrew Jennings: Did you conduct any experiments in the guest bedroom?

Thomas Kieran: Yes, I did.

Narrator 2: This revelation startles the prosecution attorneys, who were unaware of any such experiments.

Andrew Jennings: Please describe the experiment.

Thomas Kieran: I had my assistant, who is taller than Abby Borden, lie on the floor. Then I went downstairs and came up the stairs to determine if he could be seen. As I came up the stairs I could not see him, even though I knew he was there.

Andrew Jennings: Could you see his feet from any position on the stairs?

Thomas Kieran: I could not.

Narrator 1: The prosecution wanted to establish that Lizzie had lied when she claimed she didn't see Abby's body. The courtroom erupts at Kieran's revelation. Moody and the other prosecuting attorney, Hosea Knowlton, exchange worried looks. Their own witness had hurt their case.

Narrator 2: The prosecution questions John Morse and various neighbors. The treasurer of the Union Savings Bank, which Andrew had owned, testifies that Andrew died without leaving a will. Hosea Knowlton calls Bridget Sullivan to the stand. Bridget describes how she let in Mr. Borden that morning.

Hosea Knowlton: After you let Mr. Borden in, what happened?

Bridget Sullivan: I heard Miss Lizzie laugh upstairs.

Hosea Knowlton: Then what happened?

Bridget Sullivan: Miss Lizzie came down. After she started ironing she asked me if I might go out and told me that Mrs. Borden had gone out on a sick call. She said there was a dress goods sale at Sargent's and I said I would go there.

Hosea Knowlton: What do you do next?

Bridget Sullivan: I went up to my room.

Narrator 1: Bridget then describes the discovery of the body and how she was sent to Dr. Bowen's.

Hosea Knowlton: Did you ask Lizzie about her whereabouts?

Bridget Sullivan: When I came back, I said, "Miss Lizzie, where was you? Didn't I leave the screen door hooked?" She said, "I was out in the backyard and heard a groan and came in and the screen door was wide open."

Narrator 2: Attorneys for both sides relentlessly question Bridget. She leaves the stand exhausted and frightened.

Scene 6

Narrator 1: During the inquest, Dr. Seabury Bowen had testified previously that Lizzie had worn a drab, calico dress. Moody questions Dr. Bowen regarding the dress.

William Moody: What was the color of the dress that the defendant was wearing on the morning of the murders?

Dr. Bowen: The color is indefinite.

William Moody: Did it appear to be a drab-colored dress as you testified before?

Dr. Bowen: It was an ordinary, unattractive, common dress that I did not notice especially.

Narrator 2: Moody shows Bowen a blue silk dress.

William Moody: Is this the dress she had on that morning?

Dr. Bowen: I don't know, sir.

William Moody: What color do you call this?

Dr. Bowen: I should call it dark blue.

Narrator 1: Moody has succeeded in implying that this was not the dress Lizzie had worn that morning—and that perhaps the one she burned was. Moody then leads Dr. Bowen through a description of the events of the morning. Melvin O. Adams, attorney for the defense, then questions Dr. Bowen about the sedative he prescribed for Lizzie.

Melvin O. Adams: Did you prescribe a sedative for the defendant?

Dr. Bowen: Yes, sir.

Melvin O. Adams: What was it?

Dr. Bowen: Sulphate of morphine.

Melvin O. Adams: Did you change the morphine?

Dr. Bowen: I did not change the medicine, but I doubled the dose.

Melvin O. Adams: How long did Lizzie Borden have the morphine?

Dr. Bowen: All the time through her arrest and the hearing.

Melvin O. Adams: Does not morphine given in double doses somewhat affect the memory and give people hallucinations?

Dr. Bowen: Yes, sir.

Narrator 2: The defense has successfully implied that Lizzie's contradictory answers may have been caused by medication. The next witness is neighbor Adelaide Churchill who describes the events of the morning. The prosecution establishes that Lizzie had been wearing a light-blue calico print with a dark blue diamond pattern. Then George D. Robinson cross-examines Adelaide.

George D. Robinson: You had been with Miss Lizzie all the time?

Adelaide Churchill: Yes, sir.

George D. Robinson: Did you see any blood on her dress?

Adelaide Churchill: No, sir.

George D. Robinson: You were right over her, fanning her?

Adelaide Churchill: Yes, sir.

George D. Robinson: Did you see blood on her hands? On her face? On her hair?

Adelaide Churchill: No, sir.

Narrator 1: The next witness is Alice Russell, the one who caused Lizzie's indictment with her testimony about the burned dress. She describes how Lizzie had described Abby and Andrew's illnesses the night before the murders. Then Moody brings up the burning of the dress.

William Moody: What happened on Sunday morning after the murders?

Alice Russell: I was visiting the Borden household. Lizzie had a dress in her hand and

Emma asked, "What are you going to do with that?" Lizzie replied, "I am going to burn this old thing up—it is covered with paint."

William Moody: What did you say to her?

Alice Russell: I said, "I wouldn't let anybody see me do that, Lizzie."

William Moody: Did you talk with her again about it?

Alice Russell: Yes, after I was questioned during the investigation. I told her and Emma, "I am afraid, Lizzie, the worst thing you could have done was to burn that dress. I have been asked about your dresses."

William Moody: What did she say?

Alice Russell: She said, "Oh, what made you let me do it? Why didn't you tell me?"

William Moody: Please describe the dress she burned.

Alice Russell: It was light blue, with a dark blue figure on it.

Narrator 2: During the cross-examination, Miss Russell testifies that she saw no blood on the dress.

Scene 7

Narrator 1: After inconclusive testimony about the identification of the murder weapon, the prosecution tries to enter into evidence of Lizzie's contradictory testimony at the inquest. The three justices call a one-day recess to consider the admissibility of her statements. The justices conclude that Lizzie's statements are inadmissible.

Narrator 2: Dr. William Dolan testifies that Abby had died at least an hour before Andrew, and describes the total of twenty-nine blows to the victims' heads. Dr. Edward Wood, a professor of chemistry from Harvard, testifies that, after such a bludgeoning, the weapon and the person who performed the murders would be spattered with blood. He also states that no poison was present in the victims' stomachs. The prosecution rests its case.

Narrator 1: Andrew Jennings opens for the defense.

Andrew Jennings: Members of the jury, today a young woman, who led an honorable, spotless life, has been accused of a crime that has shocked the world. You do not have to decide how this brutal deed was done or who did it. All you have to do is decide whether it can be proven beyond a reasonable doubt that Lizzie Borden is guilty. There are two kinds of evidence—direct evidence and circumstantial evidence. In this case, there is not one particle of direct evidence against Lizzie Borden. There is not a spot of blood. There is not a weapon connected with her. The only evidence we have seen is merely circumstantial.

Narrator 2: Jennings emphasizes the role of reasonable doubt and that the jurors must consider the weapon, motive, opportunity, and conduct and appearance of the defendant.

Andrew Jennings: The government has not produced a weapon or a motive. There was nothing between the defendant and her father that would cause her to do this wicked act. And was Miss Lizzie the only person who could have committed the crime? No.

Narrator 1: Lizzie cries into a handkerchief while Jennings continues.

Andrew Jennings: You will learn that there were strangers seen about the Borden house around this time. We shall show you that Lizzie was in the barn. As for the burned dress, Miss Lizzie did burn it—but in broad daylight with witnesses around. After you hear all the evidence, you must decide whether the government has satisfactorily proved beyond a reasonable doubt that the defendant killed not only her stepmother, but also her beloved and loving father.

Narrator 2: The defense calls a variety of witnesses from the neighborhood who testify that a strange man was seen in the neighborhood about the time of the murders. Mark Chase, proprietor of a livery stable, testifies that he saw a horse and buggy parked in front of the Borden's house for at least an hour that morning. Then a key witness is called—Emma Borden.

Andrew Jennings: Has your sister Lizzie always lived with you?

Emma Borden: Yes, sir.

Andrew Jennings: Yourself, your father, Miss Lizzie, and Mrs. Borden?

Emma Borden: Yes, sir.

Andrew Jennings: Did your father wear a ring upon his finger?

Emma Borden: Yes, sir.

Andrew Jennings: Was or was that not the only article of jewelry which he wore?

Emma Borden: Yes, sir. He received it from my sister Lizzie.

Andrew Jennings: Did he constantly wear it?

Emma Borden: Yes, sir. It was the only jewelry he ever wore. It was on his finger when he was buried.

Narrator 1: Jennings has established the strong relationship that Andrew had with Lizzie. He then questions Emma about the light blue dress with the dark blue diamond pattern, and the fact that Lizzie had burned the dress.

Andrew Jennings: Where was the dress on the Saturday when the police were searching the house?

Emma Borden: I went to hang up a dress that I had been wearing. There was no nail to hang my dress. I noticed this dress. It was soiled and badly faded. It couldn't have been used for anything else.

Andrew Jennings: Did you say anything to your sister?

Emma Borden: I said, "You have not destroyed that old dress yet—why don't you get rid of it?"

Andrew Jennings: Tell us all that happened on Sunday morning.

Emma Borden: I was washing dishes and I heard my sister say, "I think I shall burn this old dress." I said, "Why don't you?" or "You had better" or something like that. I continued washing the dishes and did not see her burn it.

Andrew Jennings: Were other people around?

Emma Borden: Yes, there were police officers and Miss Russell.

Andrew Jennings: Did Miss Russell say anything about not burning the dress?

Emma Borden: Not then, but she said that on Monday. She told us then that she'd told the detective that a dress was missing. She said she had told him a falsehood.

Andrew Jennings: Did you hear her say that the dress shouldn't be burned?

Emma Borden: I did not.

Narrator 2: Jennings wanted to establish more confusion about the dress, which Emma provided by tainting Alice Russell's testimony. Hosea Knowlton conducts the cross-examination.

Hosea Knowlton: Did your father give some property to Mrs. Borden's sister?

Emma Borden: Yes, he did.

Hosea Knowlton: Did that make some trouble in the family?

Emma Borden: Yes, sir.

Hosea Knowlton: Did you complain to your father?

Emma Borden: Yes, sir. Father gave us Grandfather's house on Ferry Street.

Hosea Knowlton: Did your sister have a cordial relationship with your stepmother?

Emma Borden: Yes, sir.

Hosea Knowlton: Did you?

Emma Borden: No, sir.

Hosea Knowlton: How did Lizzie address your stepmother before the murders?

Emma Borden: As Mrs. Borden.

Narrator 1: Knowlton repeatedly questions Emma about prior conflicting testimony at the inquest. Emma often states that she doesn't remember what she previously said. She remains composed throughout the testimony. She admits to continuing to resent the gift of the property to Mrs. Borden's sister.

Narrator 2: Knowlton finishes his cross-examination by establishing that each family member had a waterproof raincoat—one that could have been worn during the murder to protect Lizzie's dress.

Narrator 1: The defense rests its case after its last witness.

Scene 8

Narrator 2: George D. Robinson begins the summation for the defense.

George D. Robinson: This was a diabolical crime and we must find someone equal to that crime. Here was a man who wore but one ring, one given to him by Lizzie when she was a little girl. He loved her and that ring is a symbol of that love. . . . There is no direct evidence against Miss Borden. There is no weapon—all the police of Fall River searched the Borden house, and they could not find the hatchet that killed the Bordens. There was not a spot of blood on Lizzie or her clothing. Every witness has testified to that fact.

Narrator 1: Robinson then summarizes the conflicting testimony and lack of evidence.

George D. Robinson: Miss Lizzie said she was in the barn for twenty or thirty minutes. Later she said she was in the yard. Couldn't that be true? She would go through the yard to get to the barn. They say she murdered Mr. Borden for his money. I ask you, has this been proved?

Narrator 2: Robinson reviews the witnesses who claim to have seen a stranger in the area before challenging the jury.

George D. Robinson: Look at Miss Lizzie. To find her guilty, you must believe she is a fiend. Does she look it? Please give us your verdict of not guilty so that the defendant may go home.

Narrator 1: Hosea Knowlton gives the closing argument for the prosecution.

Hosea Knowlton: This was a terrible crime and it is hard to believe that a woman did it. But don't forget, gentlemen, women are humans like us. And the evidence makes it impossible for us not to believe that this woman did this terrible crime. Think about the morning of the murder. Do you believe for a moment that those blows could have been struck without Mrs. Borden groaning or screaming? That she could have fallen without noise? Was Lizzie in the passageway when the assassin came in? Was she in her room when that heavy body fell to the floor? She alone knows. We do know that when Bridget went out to wash the windows, she left this poor woman in the house with the only enemy she had in the world.

Narrator 2: Knowlton goes on to explore the impossibility of anyone getting into the house without Lizzie's knowing about it. Then he admits that the lack of blood on Lizzie is puzzling.

Hosea Knowlton: How could she have avoided the spattering of her dress with blood if she committed these crimes? I cannot answer it. *You* cannot answer it, but there are many ways to protect a dress. *You* are neither murderers nor women.

Remember, there was no peace or harmony in this family. The family did not eat together. I admire Miss Emma's loyalty. She must come to her sister's rescue, so she tells us that family relations were peaceful. But we know they were not. She tells us she told her sister to destroy the dress, a different story from Miss Russell's. After the murders, everyone asked Lizzie the same question: Where were you when your father was killed? She said she had been in the barn for thirty minutes getting a piece of iron for sinkers—on a miserably hot day, just as her father was being killed. Show us proof.

Narrator 1: Knowlton wraps up his summation with a strong argument for conviction.

Hosea Knowlton: After finding her father murdered, Lizzie never cried out for help. She stood inside the screen door and asked Bridget to go get Dr. Bowen. There is the mystery about the burning of the dress. And the mysterious, unknown assassin who did the murders, coming in through a locked door and moving from room to room with no traces of blood in the hallways or on the stairs. The assassin knew that Bridget would be washing the windows or would be upstairs asleep. The assassin also knew that Mrs. Borden would be upstairs and that Lizzie would later go to the barn.

This case has all the elements of crime: hatred, malice, falsehood, and impossible alibis. We have contradictory stories that cannot be verified. What is the defense? Nothing, I say again, nothing.

Narrator 2: The chief justice, Josiah Blaisdell, then turns to Lizzie.

Josiah Blaisdell: Lizzie Andrew Borden, although you have been fully heard by counsel, it is your privilege to add any words that you desire to say in person to the jury. You now have the opportunity.

Narrator 1: Lizzie rises and looks at the jurors.

Lizzie Borden: I am innocent.

Narrator 2: Associate Justice Justin Dewey delivers the instruction to the jurors. He explains that the government must show that the defendant had motives and cautions them about evaluating testimony about conversations. Then he addresses the role of circumstantial evidence.

Justin Dewey: In this case, no witnesses testified to seeing the defendant commit the crime. This is a legal and not unusual way of proving a criminal case, and juries may find a person guilty of murder upon circumstantial evidence alone. You must decide what facts have been proved and what conclusions can be drawn from the facts. Look at the matter from one side. Then look at it from the other. Never assume beforehand that the defendant is guilty.

Narrator 1: Judge Dewey reviews the conflicting testimony, noting that defendants often change their statements over time. He reviews the arguments of the opposing attorneys. He points out that Lizzie was not expected to testify in her own behalf and to draw no conclusions from that decision. He concludes:

Justin Dewey: If, after weighing the evidence carefully, you are convinced beyond a reasonable doubt of the defendant's guilt, you must return a verdict of guilty. If the evidence does not convince you beyond a reasonable doubt, even a strong probability of guilt, you must return a verdict of not guilty. The case is now committed into your hands.

Narrator 2: And now, you the audience must weigh the facts as you have heard them. As in all murder trials, you must agree upon your verdict. Did Lizzie Borden murder her stepmother and her father?

Scene 9

Narrator 1: The jury begins their deliberations on Tuesday, June 20, 1893, on the thirteenth day of the trial at 3:24 P.M. One hour and six minutes later the foreman rings the bell announcing that a verdict has been reached. Lizzie stands up. The clerk asks for a verdict.

Foreman: We have a verdict. *Not guilty.*

Narrator 2: Lizzie grasps the rail, sobbing uncontrollably. The courtroom erupts in surprise and cheers. The three judges do not try to quiet the room. Emma moves forward and takes Lizzie in her arms. Within an hour Emma and Lizzie leave for Fall River.

Narrator 1: Lizzie and Emma move into a large house within five weeks. The murderer is never found. Many people believe that Lizzie benefited from a strong defense and the exclusion of her previous conflicting testimony. However, other people are suspected of killing the Bordens. Listen to Emma and Bridget describe some of the rumors.

Emma: Some people claim that I killed them. There was the mysterious carriage outside our house that morning. I would have had plenty of time, according to these people, to drive there, kill my father and stepmother, and return to Fairhaven.

Bridget Sullivan: Other people think that I killed the Bordens, and that the sisters paid me off. Mrs. Borden mistreated me, that's for sure. Imagine making someone wash windows in that heat after vomiting breakfast. If I had gone on to some rich life, maybe that theory would be credible. But was my life rich? Hardly.

Emma: Other people think that Lizzie and I worked together, so that we were sure we'd inherit everything. Neither of us married, although there were many years when we didn't even speak to each other. It is true that I had promised our *real* mother that I'd take care of Lizzie. But, do we look like murderers?

Bridget Sullivan: Another theory is that I helped the sisters cover up the murders. If that were the case, it seems to me that I'd have been in their employ the rest of their lives, living in comfort, right? They lived in a pretty grand house. They may have fallen out with each other, but it seems odd that they died within ten days of each other.

Lizzie Borden: And it could be that I really did get away with murder . . .

4

"Say It Ain't So"

The State of Illinois vs. Eddie Cicotte et al.
The White Sox Scandal of 1919

Joseph "Shoeless Joe" Jackson, outfielder with the Chicago White Sox. AP Photo.

INTRODUCTION

The world had rarely seen better baseball players than those in Charles Comiskey's White Sox club. In spite of their fine record, the team was one of the worst paid in existence. Prompted by frustration at their low salaries and essentially lifetime contracts, members of the team conspired to throw the World Series in 1919. After these events, the public began referring to the team as the Black Sox, and the scandal is still often referred to as "The Black Sox Scandal." The story is far more complex than this script can explore, especially concerning the double-crossing by the gamblers who were involved. However, the script provides the context for the team members' motivations and a glimpse of the trial that followed their exposure.

PRESENTATION SUGGESTIONS

Because this story is dominated by male characters (due to the state of the baseball field at the time), female readers might consider assuming the attorney's roles. Suggestions for costumes include baseball shirts for the players, flamboyant clothing for the gamblers, and suits for the attorneys. Because there are so many readers, the attorneys may wait offstage until the final scenes. Alternatively, use tiers of risers, with the ball players in the front row, the judge and attorneys in the top row, and all other characters in the middle row. Baseball props, such as mitts or bats, could be placed on stage.

RELATED BOOK

Asinof, Eliot. *Eight Men Out: The Black Sox and the 1919 World Series*. New York: Henry Holt, 1987.

THE STATE OF ILLINOIS VS. EDDIE CICOTTE ET AL.

CHARACTERS

Narrator 1

Oscar "Happy" Felsch, *defensive outfielder*

Eddie Cicotte, *pitcher*

"Shoeless" Joe Jackson, *hitter*

Arnold "Chick" Gandil, *first baseman*

Charles Swede Risberg, *shortstop*

Claude Williams, *pitcher*

Narrator 2

Fred McMullin, *utility infielder*

Buck Weaver, *third baseman*

Joseph "Sport" Sullivan, *gambler*

Arnold Rothstein, *gambler and financier*

William "Kid" Gleason, *club manager*

Charles Comiskey, *owner of the White Sox ball club*

Hartley L. Replogle, *Assistant State's Attorney*

Boy

George Gorman, *prosecuting attorney*

William "Sleepy" Burns, *gambler*

Thomas Nash, *defense attorney*

Judge Hugo Friend

Edward Prindeville, *prosecuting attorney*

Ben Short, *defense attorney*

Michael Ahearn, *defense attorney*

Jury Foreman

"Say It Ain't So"

State of Illinois vs. Eddie Cicotte et al.
The White Sox Scandal of 1919

Scene 1

Narrator 1: On a summer day in 1919, eight members of the Chicago White Sox, one of the finest baseball teams in the United States, gather in a hotel room after a game.

Oscar "Happy" Felsch: You pitched a great game, Eddie. I think you're going to beat your record from 1917, when you won twenty-eight games.

Eddie Cicotte: Thanks, Happy. It was okay.

"Shoeless" Joe Jackson: Just "okay"? You're the best, Eddie. Why, I heard Comiskey Park had record attendance today. Who do you think they come to watch?

Eddie Cicotte: Doesn't do us much good whether the fans come out or not.

Arnold "Chick" Gandil: What do you mean?

Eddie Cicotte: Look, we're one of the worst paid teams in the nation, no matter how much money Charles Comiskey rakes in. He owns the club—he owns us. And he sure owns the money.

Charles Swede Risberg: At least you guys get paid more than Claude and me.

Claude Williams: That's right. At our measly salary, we can barely cover our travel expenses.

Narrator 2: It's true that the White Sox players get extremely low salaries. Risberg, Williams, and Fred McMullin receive $3,000 a year. Gandil and Felsch get $4,000. Buck Weaver, one of the finest third basemen in the nation, Jackson, one of baseball's greatest hitters, and Cicotte earn approximately $6,000.

Fred McMullin: We don't even get the same as the other teams for our food allowance. Who can eat on $3 per day? Everyone else gets at least $4.

Charles Swede Risberg: What really gets to me is that Comiskey puts on lavish feasts for the reporters. You'd think they were winning the games.

Buck Weaver: Well, there's not a lot we can do about it. We can't complain to the press because Comiskey treats them so well. We can't get out of our contracts. The club can renew them forever. We either take what he offers or we don't play. Period. And I just can't imagine doing anything else but playing ball. It's my life.

Fred McMullin: I know. I love the game too. But it's hard to take such lousy pay and conditions when players on other teams that aren't doing half as well as us get paid twice as much.

Claude Williams: The only person getting rich is Charles Comiskey.

Arnold "Chick" Gandil: And the bookies.

"Shoeless" Joe Jackson: That's the truth. You know, even factory workers have it better than us. They can strike for better working conditions. They can work for someone else.

Claude Williams: Not us. If we walk away from the team after signing a contract, we're finished. No pay. And no chances to go to another team. Yet if we get injured, they can dump us—in ten days.

"Shoeless" Joe Jackson: Wait a minute. I was told that they weren't putting that clause in.

Oscar "Happy" Felsch: It's in mine. Didn't you read your contract?

"Shoeless" Joe Jackson: You know I don't read all that well. I took their word.

Buck Weaver: Well, I'm telling you boys, it doesn't matter. Gleason's a good manager, but when he complained to Comiskey, he got nowhere. We're stuck, so there's no use grousing about it. Look, we're playing the greatest game in the world. We won the World Series last year and with Eddie's pitching and Joe's hitting—well, we'll win it again this year. And Comiskey's promised a bonus.

Arnold "Chick" Gandil: Yeah, we've heard that before. All we got for our bonus last time was a case of cheap champagne. It didn't even have bubbles. There's got to be a way to get what we've got coming to us. . . .

Scene 2

Narrator 1: Just three weeks before the World Series is to begin, Joseph "Sport" Sullivan walks into Boston's Hotel Buckminster. Sullivan, a bookmaker and gambler, picks up the house phone and asks to be connected to Chick Gandil.

Narrator 2: Sullivan had befriended Gandil years ago, learning valuable tidbits about the players. Although the conversations started innocently, Sullivan was soon using the information to his benefit. Just knowing that a certain pitcher might not play a game could mean huge winnings at gambling centers across the United States.

Narrator 1: Now, as Sullivan goes to Gandil's room, he wonders why Gandil has summoned him. Gandil doesn't waste time getting to the point.

Arnold "Chick" Gandil: You know that the World Series is coming up.

Joseph "Sport" Sullivan: Sure. The White Sox should take it easily again.

Arnold "Chick" Gandil: I have something else in mind. I've had it with lousy pay, crummy hotels, and empty promises. I think I can make sure you make big money on the game.

Joseph "Sport" Sullivan: I'm listening.

Arnold "Chick" Gandil: I think I can get enough players on board to guarantee the White Sox will lose.

Joseph "Sport" Sullivan: Why are you coming to me with this?

Arnold "Chick" Gandil: You're the only one I know who has the kind of resources to bankroll it. I want $80,000 to pull it off.

Joseph "Sport" Sullivan: And you really think you can?

Arnold "Chick" Gandil: Practically positive. If you could have heard the guys a few weeks ago—well, I think I can get eight to come on board.

Joseph "Sport" Sullivan: What about Cicotte? You can't do it without him.

Narrator 2: Gandil knew all along that he needed Cicotte. He'd laid the groundwork, talking privately to Cicotte for weeks about throwing the Series. Cicotte had repeatedly refused, even though he had huge mortgage payments on a farm he'd just bought. Finally, on the train to Boston, Cicotte had told Gandil quietly that he'd throw the Series for $10,000, delivered before the Series began.

Arnold "Chick" Gandil: Don't worry about Cicotte. He's in.

Joseph "Sport" Sullivan: Well, this has possibilities, but I need to think about it. Let me get back to you.

Arnold "Chick" Gandil: Don't wait too long.

Narrator 1: As Sullivan leaves the hotel, he thinks about Gandil's proposal. On the one hand, it is a scheme that makes a mockery of the most popular sport in the nation. On the other hand, an opportunity to make a huge profit has dropped in his lap. He isn't worried about getting in serious trouble—he has plenty of connections. And there is always the chance he can pull it off.

Scene 3

Narrator 2: Feeling confident that he will get the money, Gandil goes into action. He starts with Claude Williams after a Yankees game in New York City.

Arnold "Chick" Gandil: Claude, let's talk for a minute.

Claude Williams: Sure. What's up?

Arnold "Chick" Gandil: Listen, I've got a way for us to make a lot of money on the Series. Guaranteed.

Claude Williams: What are you talking about?

Arnold "Chick" Gandil: All we have to do is make sure we don't win.

Claude Williams: What are you talking about? Throwing the Series? Have you lost your mind?

Arnold "Chick" Gandil: It's all set. Doesn't matter to me whether you're in or not. But if you pass this up, you'll have nothing. You might as well get in on the action.

Claude Williams: Is Cicotte in?

Arnold "Chick" Gandil: Yes.

Claude Williams: Let me think about it.

Narrator 1: Now Gandil needed to make sure he had a few others. He completed his list: George "Buck" Weaver, Oscar "Happy" Felsch, "Shoeless" Joe Jackson, Fred McMullin, and Swede Risberg. The eight men met after dinner on September 21, 1919.

Arnold "Chick" Gandil: I know all of you are sick of winning games for Comiskey and never getting paid fairly for it. Well, I've decided it's time to do something about it. Here's the deal. I met with "Sport" Sullivan and told him that for $80,000—in advance—we'd guarantee that the White Sox will lose the World Series.

Buck Weaver: Are you crazy?

Arnold "Chick" Gandil: No, just practical. Look, we'll never see this kind of money again. All you have to do is say you're in. We'll get paid the money. Then the bookmakers will work with us on the details, like the sequence of losses. We can't look like we're deliberately losing, of course. The best part—no one gets hurt.

Buck Weaver: Eddie, what about you? I can't believe you'd go for this.

Eddie Cicotte: Buck, look at how Comiskey treated me after he'd promised me a $10,000 bonus for breaking my winning streak two years ago. As soon as I got close, he benched me. I'm in.

Arnold "Chick" Gandil: Well, what about the rest of you?

Oscar "Happy" Felsch: I'm in.

"Shoeless" Joe Jackson: Me too.

Williams, Risberg, McMullin: Okay.

Arnold "Chick" Gandil: Buck?

Buck Weaver: Sorry, fellas. I just can't do it.

Scene 4

Narrator 2: While Gandil gets his conspirators lined up, rumors of a fix spreads among the gamblers. William "Sleepy" Burns hears the rumors and decides to try to get in on the action. He meets with Gandil and Cicotte and later with several members of the team. They discuss a fee of $100,000.

Narrator 1: As opening day approaches, both Burns and "Sport" Sullivan scramble to raise the money. They know of one man who would probably bankroll it—Arnold Rothstein, a sportsman and professional gambler with a talent for making money. Burns approaches him first, but Rothstein refuses to meet with him. Rothstein does meet with Sullivan, a man he respects.

Joseph "Sport" Sullivan: Mr. Rothstein, I have a business proposition for you.

Arnold Rothstein: Is this about the Series?

Joseph "Sport" Sullivan: What have you heard?

Arnold Rothstein: Just rumors. Are they true?

Joseph "Sport" Sullivan: They could be . . . but the players need $80,000.

Arnold Rothstein: You sure you can pull this off?

Joseph "Sport" Sullivan: It's in the bag—I have eight players ready.

Arnold Rothstein: That's a lot of people to keep quiet. On the other hand, it will be hard to find the truth with so many people involved. I tell you what. You'll get $40,000 now to get this started. If the Series goes as planned, you'll get the other half.

Joseph "Sport" Sullivan: Thanks, Mr. Rothstein. You won't be disappointed.

Arnold Rothstein: I hope not. You'll be hearing from my associates about the arrangements. Now, take the money and do your part.

Narrator 2: With forty crisp $1000 bills in his pocket, Sullivan decides to string the players along with $10,000 and use $30,000 for bets. After making his wager, he faces Gandil.

Arnold "Chick" Gandil: Only $10,000? That wasn't our agreement.

Joseph "Sport" Sullivan: You're lucky to get it. There are so many rumors out there that the odds are already dropping. Someone's been talking. Or . . . maybe you guys are playing with someone else . . .

Arnold "Chick" Gandil: You know better than that. But Cicotte needs $10,000 up front and without him, this will fall apart. What am I going to tell the others?

Joseph "Sport" Sullivan: Tell them to keep their mouths shut!

Arnold "Chick" Gandil: You've got your nerve! I ought to tell the guys to forget it.

Joseph "Sport" Sullivan: Just try it, if you don't want to ever play ball again.

Narrator 1: The men argue angrily. Then they realize there's no going back. The Series begins in two days. Later that night, Gandil slips $10,000 under Cicotte's pillow.

Scene 5

Narrator 2: Betting is heavy on opening day of the 1919 World Series, October 1, as the Chicago White Sox face off against the Cincinnati Reds. Telegrams of rumors of a fix

THE STATE OF ILLINOIS VS. EDDIE CICOTTE ET AL. 51

have reached William "Kid" Gleason, the manager, who finds it hard to believe that his players would ruin such a great season. To Gleason's dismay, Cicotte's pitching is inconsistent. The White Sox lose to the Reds, 9–1.

Narrator 1: That night Gleason confronts Cicotte and Risberg, who are enjoying themselves in the lobby of the hotel.

William "Kid" Gleason: Cicotte! Risberg! What are you laughing at? You think you can kid me? You think I don't see what's going on out there?

Narrator 2: Nearly one hundred observers in the lobby listen in shock. Gleason leaves and finds Charles Comiskey, the team owner.

William "Kid" Gleason: Charles, look at these telegrams I've gotten—all from gamblers warning me of a fix.

Charles Comiskey: What did you think of today's game?

William "Kid" Gleason: I've never seen them play like such a bunch of losers.

Charles Comiskey: Do you think it's true? They're throwing the Series?

William "Kid" Gleason: I'm not sure. I just can't believe it. How could they do that?

Charles Comiskey: Well, keep your eyes and ears open.

Narrator 1: The next day the Cincinnati Reds' fans are stunned at the second win. The White Sox players who are not in on the fix are increasingly frustrated, and tempers are hot. Weaver, who had refused to go along with the fix, is playing his best. But he keeps quiet.

Narrator 2: Meanwhile, Sullivan stalls the promised payoffs. Without money coming in, the players decide to teach the gamblers a lesson—they win game 3. The money starts to trickle in again. They lose games 4 and 5, and when the money doesn't arrive again, they win games 6 and 7. Rothstein tells Sullivan he doesn't want the Series to go to game 9. Sullivan sends a man only known as "Harry" to pay Claude Williams a persuasive visit. The White Sox lose the Series with game 8.

Scene 6

Narrator 1: Except for the bookmakers and gamblers, Chick Gandil profits the most from the fix. From the $80,000, he distributes $45,000 among the other players, leaving $35,000 for himself. He leaves for California as quickly as possible.

Narrator 2: "Shoeless" Joe Jackson is not so quick to leave. His conscience is already bothering him, and he asks to speak with Charles Comiskey, who refuses to see him. Troubled, he leaves for Savannah, Georgia, for the winter.

Narrator 1: By spring of 1920, baseball fans are ready for the new season. Then the pressure starts on the tainted players. Fred McMullin is contacted by the gamblers and told to lose a game. A pattern of wins and losses begins, and by September, Judge

McDonald of Cook County, Illinois, investigates charges that gamblers fixed a game in August. He also recommends an investigation of the 1919 World Series. A grand jury convenes and pressure mounts. Cicotte, feeling miserable and guilty, agrees to tell the grand jury the truth. Assistant State's Attorney Hartley L. Replogle interrogates him during the hearing.

Hartley L. Replogle: Tell us what happened, Mr. Cicotte.

Eddie Cicotte: I don't know why I did it . . . I must have been crazy. Gandil was at me for weeks before the Series began. I needed the money for the wife and the kids. Gandil was mixed up with gamblers before he was a ballplayer. That's how he got the idea to fix the Series. Eight of us got together in my room to talk about it. We decided we could get away with it.

Hartley L. Repogle: Tell us about the pay.

Eddie Cicotte: We each talked about the money alone with Gandil. I told him I needed $10,000 in advance and I got it. I sold out the other boys. Sold them out to pay off a mortgage on a farm for the wife and kids.

Hartley L. Repogle: Tell us how you can throw a game.

Eddie Cicotte: It's easy. Just a slight hesitation on the players' part will let a man get to base or make a run. I could just lob the ball over the plate—a baby could hit 'em. Sometimes I'd be slow enough to prevent a double play. It didn't look crooked on my part. All the runs scored against me were due to my own deliberate errors.

Hartley L. Repogle: Do you have anything else to say?

Eddie Cicotte: I've lived a thousand years in the last twelve months. Now I've lost everything, job, reputation. My friends all bet on the Sox. I had to double-cross them. I'm through with baseball. I'm going to lose myself if I can and start life over again.

Narrator 2: Knowing that Cicotte has opened up to the grand jury is the last straw for "Shoeless" Joe Jackson, whose conscience had been troubling him all year. He calls Judge McDonald and says he is ready to talk to the grand jury.

Hartley L. Repogle: Did anyone pay you money to help throw that Series in favor of Cincinnati?

"Shoeless" Joe Jackson: They did.

Hartley L. Repogle: How much did they pay?

"Shoeless" Joe Jackson: They promised me $20,000 and paid me $5,000.

Hartley L. Repogle: Who promised you $20,000?

"Shoeless" Joe Jackson: "Chick" Gandil.

Hartley L. Repogle: What did you say when you never got the money?

THE STATE OF ILLINOIS VS. EDDIE CICOTTE ET AL.   53

"Shoeless" Joe Jackson: Gandil said we got double-crossed by the gamblers. I don't think Gandil was crossed as much as he crossed us. I think he kept the majority of it.

Hartley L. Repogle: Didn't you think you should tell Comiskey about it?

"Shoeless" Joe Jackson: I tried to get out of it. But Chick Gandil said it wouldn't be good for me if I pulled out.

Hartley L. Repogle: Let's talk about the games. Did you see any fake plays that would help throw the game?

"Shoeless" Joe Jackson: Only by Cicotte.

Hartley L. Repogle: Did you make any intentional errors yourself?

"Shoeless" Joe Jackson: No, sir, not during the whole Series.

Hartley L. Repogle: Did you bat to win?

"Shoeless" Joe Jackson: Yes, sir.

Hartley L. Repogle: Were you angry that you got $5,000 when you expected $20,000?

"Shoeless" Joe Jackson: No, I was ashamed of myself.

Narrator 1: After extensive questioning about the fix and the current season, the questioning ends. Jackson, weary and defeated, leaves the courtroom. A small boy clutches at his sleeve and tags along after him.

Boy: *(pleading)* Say it ain't so, Joe. Say it ain't so.

"Shoeless" Joe Jackson: Yes, kid, I'm afraid it is.

Boy: Well, I never would've thought it.

Scene 7

Narrator 2: Within days, Claude Williams also comes forward and confesses to the grand jury. Although Comiskey doesn't hear the confessions, he dictates the telegram that suspends the eight players from the club, knowing that this will cost Chicago the pennant.

Charles Comiskey: *(dictating)* You and each of you are hereby notified of your indefinite suspension. . . . If you are innocent of any wrongdoing, you will be reinstated. If you are guilty, you will be retired from organized baseball for the rest of your life if I can accomplish it.

Narrator 1: The case of State of Illinois vs. Eddie Cicotte et al. opens on June 27, 1921, in the courtroom of Judge Hugo Friend. The players face a variety of charges of conspiracy, all related to defrauding the public and injuring the business of baseball, including Comiskey's profits.

Narrator 2: The first to testify is Comiskey. The defense attorneys try to demonstrate that his profits soared in spite of the loss of the Series. However, Comiskey's finances are ruled as not relevant.

Narrator 1: The prosecution calls their key witness, William "Sleepy" Burns, who had unsuccessfully tried to edge out Sport Sullivan. Burns, dressed in a green checkered suit with a lavender shirt and bow tie, takes the stand. Assistant State Attorney George Gorman questions him.

George Gorman: Mr. Burns, who did you meet with on September 18th?

William "Sleepy" Burns: Eddie Cicotte and Chick Gandil.

George Gorman: Was anything said?

William "Sleepy" Burns: Yes. Gandil said, "If I could get $100,000, I would throw the World Series!"

George Gorman: And what did you say?

William "Sleepy" Burns: I said I would see what I could do.

George Gorman: Did you meet with any others?

William "Sleepy" Burns: I met with Gandil, McMullin, Williams, Felsch, Cicotte, and Weaver the day before the Series started.

George Gorman: What did you talk about?

William "Sleepy" Burns: I told them I had the $100,000 to handle the throwing of the World Series. I also told them I had the names of the financiers.

George Gorman: Did the players make any statements concerning the order of the games to be thrown?

William "Sleepy" Burns: Gandil and Cicotte said the first two games should be thrown. They said, however, that it didn't matter to them. They would throw them in any order the financiers wanted.

Narrator 2: On cross-examination, Burns insists that he got nothing out of the deal—and that the players proposed the fix, not the gamblers. This especially disturbs Joe Jackson, who realizes he will be judged with Cicotte and Gandil. Unfortunately, all eight accused men, including Weaver who never went along with the fix, are convinced that their best defense is to stand together—and refuse to testify in their own defense.

Narrator 1: The state then shocks the court with the revelation that the signed confessions and immunity waivers of Cicotte, Jackson, and Williams have disappeared. No one seems to know what happened to them. However, the judge decides that the confessions were given voluntarily and will be admissible.

Narrator 2: The defense concentrates on implicating a variety of gamblers and middlemen used by Rothstein. None are in the courtroom. Then defense attorney Thomas Nash calls William "Kid" Gleason to the stand.

Thomas Nash: Mr. Gleason, were you at the ballpark on Tuesday morning, the day before the first game?

William "Kid" Gleason: I got there at about ten o'clock.

Thomas Nash: Were these team members practicing?

William "Kid" Gleason: Yes, they were.

Thomas Nash: Well, then these defendants could not have been meeting with Burns, could they?

William "Kid" Gleason: Not while they were practicing.

Narrator 1: This shocks the courtroom. Burns testimony was critical to the prosecution.

Thomas Nash: Mr. Gleason, from your experience, have you an opinion as to whether these defendants executed the plays during the World Series to the best of their abilities?

George Gorman: Objection!

Judge Hugo Friend: Sustained!

Narrator 2: The defense finally gets on record the fact that Comiskey's profits had nearly doubled in 1920, in spite of the loss of the Series. The defense rests its case, raising a key question: How could the players have conspired to ruin Comiskey's business if profits had almost doubled?

Scene 8

Narrator 1: The summations begin with Edward Prindeville, prosecuting attorney.

Edward Prindeville: What more convincing proof do you want than the statement by the ballplayers? Joe Jackson, Eddie Cicotte, and Claude Williams sold out the American public for a paltry $20,000. They collected the money, but they could not keep quiet. Their consciences would not let them rest. Cicotte told us of the $10,000 he got under his pillow. He admitted meeting his pals and talking over the conspiracy details. The gamblers accepted the players' terms. I say, gentlemen, that the evidence shows that a swindle and con game has been worked on the American people. The crime in this case warrants the most severe punishment of the law. The State is asking for a verdict of guilty with five years in the penitentiary and a fine of $2,000 for each defendant!

Narrator 2: Prosecutor George Gorman concludes the summation.

George Gorman: Comiskey gave these men a job. And here we find the defendants deliberately conspiring to injure and destroy his business. The public went to the game believing it was on the square. There they waited to see the great Cicotte pitch a ball game. Gentlemen, they went to see a ball game. But all they saw was a con game!

Narrator 1: Defense attorney Ben Short begins the summation for the players.

Ben Short: The State failed to establish criminal conspiracy. There had been an agreement by the defendants to take the gamblers' money, but it has not been shown that these players had any intention of defrauding the public or bringing the game into ill repute. They believed any arrangement they may have made was a secret one and would, therefore, reflect no discredit on the national pastime or injure the business of their employers, as it would never be detected!

Narrator 2: The defense then attacks the fact that Arnold Rothstein and the other gamblers were not indicted, implying that the powers controlling baseball have protected them. Michael Ahearn concludes the summation for the defense.

Michael Ahearn: Burns has been proved a liar in a score of instances. He said he talked to the ballplayers on the morning before the opening game. He lied. He makes me think of a drink of moonshine: It looks good, but when you drink, it gives you a stomachache!

Narrator 1: With these words, all that is left is for Judge Friend to deliver his charge to the jury. One statement is especially important.

Judge Hugo Friend: The State must prove that it was the intent of the ballplayers charged with conspiracy through the throwing of the World Series to defraud the public and others, and not merely to throw ball games.

Narrator 2: This is what the defense is hoping for. Nothing in the testimony supports the notion that the ballplayers intended to defraud the public. The ballplayers smile hesitantly as the jury begins its deliberations at exactly 7:52 P.M. And now, you the audience must weigh the facts as you have heard them. Are the eight ballplayers guilty—or innocent?

Scene 9

Narrator 1: Just before ten o'clock, three loud knocks on the jury-room door indicate that a verdict has been reached. Hundreds of spectators gather in the courtroom.

Judge Hugo Friend: Gentlemen of the jury, have you reached a verdict?

Jury Foreman: We have, Your Honor.

Narrator 2: The clerk hands Judge Friend a slip of paper from the foreman.

Foreman: We the jury find the defendant Claude Williams not guilty. . . .

Narrator 1: A roar goes up in the courtroom. As the foreman repeats "not guilty," hats and confetti fly in the air. Several jurors lift the players to their shoulders and parade them around the room. The players pound each other on the back.

Buck Weaver: I knew I'd be cleared. And I'm glad the public stood by me until the trial was over.

Narrator 2: The ballplayers have a celebratory dinner in an Italian restaurant near the Criminal Courts building. Coincidentally, the jurors celebrate in the next room. The groups join for a resounding party.

Narrator 1: Their celebration ends early the next morning with the arrival of the newspapers. The new Commissioner of Baseball, Judge Kenesaw Mountain Landis, has already released a statement to the press. Cicotte reads it in despair.

Eddie Cicotte: "Regardless of the verdict of juries, no player who throws a ball game, no player that undertakes or promises to throw a ball game, no player that sits in a conference with a bunch of crooked players and gamblers where the ways and means of throwing a game are discussed and does not promptly tell his club about it, will ever play professional baseball."

Narrator 2: For these eight men it was over—they never played professional baseball again.

5

A Perfect Crime

The People against Nathan Leopold, Jr.
and Richard Loeb
The Sentencing Hearing

Nathan Leopold, *far right,* and **Richard Loeb,** *second from right,* during arraignment for the kidnapping and murder of Bobby Franks, with attorney **Clarence Darrow,** *left.* AP Photo.

INTRODUCTION

In 1924, the charge of kidnapping and murder of young Bobby Franks by two wealthy, intelligent, and seemingly charming teens stunned Chicago and the nation. Richard Loeb, son of a retired Sears Roebuck vice president, was at age eighteen the youngest graduate to date at the University of Michigan. Fascinated with crime, he consumed detective novels and enjoyed fantasizing about committing the perfect crime. Nathan Leopold, passionately interested in ornithology, was already recognized at age nineteen as a leading authority on the Kirtland warbler, an endangered songbird. Although both had a variety of other friends, their friendship was considered by many to be intense and perhaps "unnatural," with Loeb identified as the manipulative leader of the two. Clarence Darrow, an outspoken opponent of the death penalty, agreed to defend the teens. He convinced the families that their best chance for keeping the youths alive was for them to plead guilty. Therefore, the case became a sentencing hearing, during which Darrow argued that the defendants receive life imprisonment. Many newspapers reprinted Darrow's entire twelve-hour summation, considered by most as an eloquent statement against capital punishment. Listeners can determine whether the sentencing was justified. Students can also discuss whether the outcome would have been different had the students been minority or underprivileged.

PRESENTATION SUGGESTIONS

In this script, the characters address the audience directly, recounting each part of the story. They do not interact with each other and should rehearse their parts so that they assume the persona of the individual they are representing. All characters should sit in chairs, standing for their readings except for the judge. The following characters should sit on one side and to the back of the stage, preferably in shadows, walking forward for their parts and then returning to their chairs: Robert Franks, Jacob Franks, and Flora Franks. Robert Crowe should sit on the same side of the stage, although facing forward near the front. Richard Loeb and Nathan Leopold should sit to one side of the stage, standing for their parts. Clarence Darrow should sit on their side of the stage. Judge John R. Caverly should sit in the center. The narrator and Howard Mayer can be on either side for balance. As in many of the historic trials, there were few women playing key roles. Consider assigning the roles of Crowe, Caverly, or Mayer to female students, reminding them that actors often assume a variety of roles, regardless of gender.

RELATED BOOK

Geis, Gilbert, and Leigh B. Bienen. *Crimes of the Century*. Boston: Northeastern University Press, 1998.

THE PEOPLE AGAINST NATHAN LEOPOLD, JR. AND RICHARD LOEB

CHARACTERS

Narrator

Robert Franks, *age fourteen, a student and the victim of the kidnapping*

Jacob Franks, *Robert's father*

Flora Franks, *Robert's mother*

Robert Crowe, *chief investigator and prosecutor*

Howard Mayer, *reporter*

Richard Loeb, *accused kidnapper and murderer of Robert Franks*

Nathan Leopold, *accused kidnapper and murderer of Robert Franks*

Clarence Darrow, *reknowned defense attorney*

John R. Caverly, *judge*

capital punishment opinion?

A Perfect Crime

The People against Nathan Leopold, Jr. and Richard Loeb
The Sentencing Hearing

Scene 1

Narrator: In this case, you will hear from the key people affected by a crime that shocked and outraged the people of Chicago—and the nation. Each will give you a piece of the puzzle. You will then try to put the pieces together to create a whole—if you can.

Robert Franks: I didn't know when I walked home from school at about five o'clock on May 21, 1924, that this would be my last day on earth. I attended the Harvard School in Chicago's Hyde Park district. I was a pretty good student and especially enjoyed being on the debate team.

I didn't recognize the gray Winton car when it pulled up alongside me, but I recognized Richard Loeb. We often played tennis together, and we were actually distant cousins. So when he asked me to get in the car to discuss a tennis racquet, I wasn't suspicious. I didn't expect to be hit on the head with a chisel or to have a cloth crammed down my throat. I didn't expect to be stripped of my clothes. I didn't expect to have hydrochloric acid poured on my body. I didn't expect to be stuffed in a concrete culvert in the Wolf Lake area.

When I was on the debate team, I argued against capital punishment. I'm not sure I'd argue against it now.

Jacob Franks: Bobby was my son. When dinnertime came on May 21, 1924, we wondered where he was, but figured he was playing tennis at the Loebs'. I didn't see him on the Loebs' tennis court, so Flora, Bobby's mother, called his friends. No one knew where he was. I called my friend, Samuel Ettelson, and we went to the school to look for Bobby.

Flora Franks: While my husband was gone, I got a phone call from a man named Johnson. I'll never forget his exact words: "Your son has been kidnapped. He is all right. There will be further news in the morning." I fainted and didn't come to until my husband and Sam got home. They went to the police that night and planned to return in the morning.

Jacob Franks: The next morning, the mailman brought a special delivery letter. It said that Bobby was well and safe and that we had to follow instructions exactly or Bobby would die. We were told to make no contact with the authorities and to put $10,000 in $20 and $50 bills in a box wrapped in white paper and sealed. It was signed by a

THE PEOPLE AGAINST NATHAN LEOPOLD, JR. AND RICHARD LOEB

"George Johnson" who promised—yes, he *promised*—that if we delivered the money, Bobby would be returned unharmed. Of course, I got the money. And, in spite of the directions, Sam called his friend, who was the chief of detectives.

Flora Franks: A reporter had been tipped off that our son had been kidnapped. He'd also heard that a body had been found. He called us and described the body, but Jacob didn't think it sounded like Bobby. Still, my brother went to see for himself.

Jacob Franks: Then this "George Johnson" called, saying he was sending a cab to take me to a drugstore on East 63rd Street.

Flora Franks: Before Jacob could leave, the phone rang again. My brother told me that the body was Bobby's. My Bobby was only fourteen years old.

Scene 2

Narrator: Robert Crowe, the chief investigator of the crime, was determined to find out who murdered young Bobby Franks.

Robert Crowe: I was in charge of the investigation. Rewards totaled $16,000, and our department was determined to find the killers of young Franks. We didn't find Bobby's clothes near the body, but we did find a pair of eyeglasses on the ground. The ransom letter was typed on an Underwood typewriter. We knew the letter had to be written by an educated and intelligent person—a dangerous combination for a criminal.

The obvious motive was greed. Someone intended to cash in on Robert Franks, a millionaire's son. We questioned three teachers from Franks's school, with no success.

The autopsy showed that Franks had died of suffocation. Wounds on his body suggested he fought with his captor. Bleeding and bruises on his forehead indicated he'd been struck with a blunt instrument.

Howard Mayer: I was a reporter on the *Evening American* newspaper and was the campus liaison for the University of Chicago. The day after the kidnapping, while I was at the Zeta Beta Tau fraternity house, Richard Loeb, a student, suggested that we try to find the drugstore that the kidnapper had told Jacob Franks to go to. Two reporters from the *Daily News* stopped by the house and went with us. We eventually got to the Van de Bogert and Ross drugstore, where we learned there had been two calls for Mr. Franks the previous day.

"This is the place!" Loeb pronounced. "This is what comes from reading detective stories!"

One of the other reporters asked Loeb if he knew Franks, and we were stunned at his smiling response. "If I were going to murder anyone, I would murder just such a cocky little jerk as Bobby Franks."

Robert Crowe: When we questioned the game warden for the Wolf Lake area, we discovered that Nathan Leopold, an avid ornithologist, often visited the area to study birds. We took Leopold to the LaSalle Hotel for questioning, and his answers were believable at first.

But there was the matter of the glasses. The prescription was common, but the frames were expensive, and they were chewed at the ends. Bobby Franks didn't wear glasses. Leopold did, but he couldn't produce his. We knew that the hinges on the glasses were sold on only three pairs of glasses in the Chicago area—all coming from one optical company. One of those three pairs belonged to Nathan Leopold.

Leopold admitted that the glasses were his and said they must have fallen out of his pocket when he was birding with some friends a few days before the kidnapping. Yet, Leopold couldn't demonstrate how the glasses might have fallen out of his pocket.

Of course, Leopold didn't know that we were questioning Richard Loeb in another room. After some reporters got hold of some study sheets that Leopold had typed on a portable typewriter and discovered that the typing on the ransom note was identical, Leopold and Loeb's stories began to unravel.

Scene 3

Richard Loeb: Nathan Leopold was my best friend. We did everything together. We had talked about kidnapping someone for a long time. We even had a plan. We loved the excitement. Six months ago we robbed my fraternity house in the middle of the night. We wore masks and came prepared with a rope to tie up anyone who might be up. We had a couple of guns and a chisel wrapped in tape in case we had to knock someone out. We stole some stuff, but it was too easy.

What we really wanted to do was commit the perfect crime. We knew we couldn't kidnap someone from our families because we'd be likely suspects. We weren't sure who it would be, but we knew it had to be someone from a rich family and someone we knew so he'd get in the car with us. We knew from the start that we'd have to murder him. Well, we couldn't have a witness, could we?

We rented a car and covered the license plate so that it would be hard to trace the vehicle. We went to our classes as usual and then put our plan into action. We considered a couple of students, but no one was quite right—then we saw Bobby Franks. I had played tennis with Bobby, so I asked him to look at a tennis racket with me. He got in the car and Nathan hit him on the head and forced a cloth down his throat. We covered him up with a rug and took off toward the Indiana border.

After a while we pulled off the road, stripped Franks, and covered him again. We needed to pass some time until dark, so we had dinner in Hammond. Then we headed to Wolf Lake. Finding the culvert [sewer or drain] was a lucky break—because we didn't want to take time to bury him. We poured some hydrochloric acid on his face and a scar so he couldn't be easily identified. On our way back, Nathan called Mr. Franks to tell him his son had been kidnapped.

Nathan Leopold: I want to make it clear that I only wanted to please Dick. As incredible as it sounds, I thought so much of the guy that I was willing to do anything—even commit murder—if he wanted it badly enough. And he wanted to do this very badly. Dick's charm was magnetic—maybe mesmerizing is the better word. He could charm anybody if he had a mind to. Yet he looked down on nearly everybody. But then there was that other side to him. He wasn't exactly immoral—it's just that right and wrong didn't exist for him. He'd do anything, and it was all a game to him. He reminded me of a kid all wrapped up in a game of cops and robbers.

I don't know why I let this go so far. I was looking forward to going to Europe with my family. I had a girlfriend, I taught four birding classes, and I was going to study law in the fall. But Dick had such a hold on me. And he was so jealous—even of the food I ate and the water I drank.

I wasn't the one who killed Bobby. Dick did that, though I suspect he's claimed I did it. But once Bobby was dead, I realized there was no turning back. After dumping the body, we threw out the chisel on the way to Dick's house. We burned the clothes that had blood on them and tried to clean up the rental car. We stayed up late playing casino.

The next day we worked out the final details for getting the ransom note delivered and collecting the money. We knew something had gone wrong when Mr. Franks didn't go to the drugstore.

I just want to say that I offer no excuse, but that I am fully convinced that neither the idea nor the act would have occurred to me had it not been for the suggestion and stimulus of Richard ~~Leopold~~ Loeb. I would not have been capable of killing Franks on my own.

Scene 4

Clarence Darrow: The families of Nathan Leopold and Richard Loeb hired Benjamin Bachrach and me to represent the young men. Once the boys signed the confessions, there was not much chance they would escape conviction. They had even helped the authorities with the collection of evidence. And they had been entirely too free with statements to their friends and the press. Why, Nathan once told a reporter that they'd rehearsed the kidnapping at least three times . . . that it was just an experiment.

It didn't take me long to realize that a guilty plea was the only chance I had to keep them alive. If they were to plead not guilty, the state of Illinois could try them in front of a jury on kidnapping charges. If they weren't convicted in that trial, they'd probably get convicted in the next trial for murder. Either conviction would likely lead to the death penalty—the public was clamoring for someone to hang.

Jacob Loeb knew that I was opposed to capital punishment and begged me to keep the boys from hanging. With a guilty plea, a judge instead of a jury would hear their case. I was pretty sure John R. Caverly would be the judge on the case. He was known to be a kindly, fair man, so I convinced the families that pleading guilty gave the boys their best shot at getting life in prison.

John R. Caverly: The case of *The People against Nathan Leopold, Jr. and Richard Loeb* opened in my courtroom on July 21, 1924. Defense Attorney Darrow spoke quietly about how no one believed that the defendants should be released, and that the defendants wanted to plead guilty. Everyone, including myself, was shocked. Everyone expected Darrow to plead them not guilty by reason of insanity.

I spoke to the boys and explained that the court could sentence them to death or to life in the penitentiary for anywhere from fourteen years to life. Both boys agreed that they understood and that they still wanted to plead guilty.

It was then that I realized I would be the only one deciding whether the boys would hang. This wasn't a decision I wanted to make.

Scene 5

Narrator: Because of the change of plea, the trial technically became a hearing and lasted nearly a month. Robert Crowe, the State's Attorney for Cook County, had conducted a thorough and professional investigation of the murder. Now he was going to prosecute the case. During the hearing he brought more than one hundred witnesses to the stand, determined to prove Loeb and Leopold's guilt, in spite of their guilty pleas. Darrow began his summation on August 22, fighting for their lives for twelve hours.

Clarence Darrow: Your honor, it has only been three months since the great responsibility of this case was assumed by my associates and myself . . . three months of great anxiety. "The motive was to get $10,000," they say. These two boys who never needed a cent killed this little boy to get $10,000? Each of the boys had all the money they needed and the boys had been raised in luxury. Yet they murdered a little boy against whom they had nothing. This case rests on money as a motive. Without money as the motive, it was a senseless act that we can't fully understand, an act of children.

Were these boys in their right minds? Here are two boys with good intellect, one eighteen and one nineteen. They sacrificed everything for a crazy scheme. Now, Your Honor, you have been a boy. I have been a boy. The best way to understand somebody else is to put yourself in his place. Is it within the realm of your imagination that a boy with all the prospects of life before him, who could choose what he wanted, would lure a young companion to his death, and take his place in the shadow of the gallows?

How insane they are I care not, whether medically or legally. They did not reason; they could not reason. They committed the most foolish, most unprovoked, most purposeless act two boys ever committed, and they put themselves where the rope is dangling above their heads.

Why did they kill little Bobby Franks?

Not for the money, not for spite, not for hate. They killed him as they might kill a spider or a fly, for the experience. They killed because they were made that way. Because somewhere in the infinite processes that go to the making up of the boy or the man, something slipped, and now those unfortunate lads sit here hated, despised, outcasts, with the community shouting for their blood.

Here are these two families, who have led honest lives. Here is Leopold's father—and this boy was the pride of his life. His son is brilliant and accomplished. The father educated him and thought that fame and position awaited him. It is a hard thing for a father to see his life's hopes crumble into dust. Should he be considered? Should Leopold's brothers be considered? Will it do society any good or make any life safer if this boy dies on the scaffold?

And Loeb—here is the faithful uncle and brother, who have watched day by day, while his father and mother are too ill to stand this strain. Shall these be taken into account?

At one time in England they hanged children seven years of age. Hanging wasn't meant as punishment. It was meant for an exhibition. If somebody committed a crime, he would be hanged by the head or the heels—it didn't matter which—at four crossroads so that everyone could see him. The rationale was that people would then be good because they had seen the gruesome result of crime and hate. We have not grown better than the ancients. We have grown more squeamish. We do not like to look at it, that is all. We have raised the age of hanging. However, of the ninety men hanged in Illinois, not one person under the age of twenty-three was hanged after pleading guilty.

We know from Dick Loeb's nurse that he loved reading detective stories. Just last year the legislature of this state ruled that boys could not read these books. Why? Because it felt that such books would produce criminal tendencies in the boys who read them. He read them day after day, even while at college. As a child he had a fantasy of heading up a band of criminals. Then he conceived the idea of a perfect crime, one that nobody could ever detect. A perfect crime.

Nathan, who is somewhat older than Dick, is a boy of remarkable mind. He is also a sort of freak—a boy without emotions, obsessed with learning. He went to college young, an intellectual machine, seeking to find out everything. At age seventeen, while healthy boys were playing baseball or doing odd jobs, he was reading Nietzsche. He became obsessed by a philosophy that scorned values by which most children are raised. He and Dick embraced it, believing they were the supermen, and that the ordinary expectations of society didn't apply to them.

The easy and the popular thing to do is to hang my clients. I know it. Men and women who do not think will applaud. The cruel and thoughtless will approve. I know Your Honor stands between the future and the past. I plead not merely for the lives of these two unfortunate lads, but for all boys and girls, for all of the young, for all of the old. I am pleading for life, understanding, charity, kindness, and the infinite mercy that considers all. I am pleading that we overcome cruelty with kindness and hatred with love.

You may hang these boys, hang them by the neck until they are dead. But in doing it you will turn your face toward the past. I hope that have done something to help human understanding, to temper justice with mercy, to overcome hate with love.

I was reading last night from the writings of the old Persian poet, Omar Khayyam. I wish it were in the hearts of all:

So I be written in the Book of Love
I do not care about that Book above.
Erase my name or write it as you will.
So I be written in the book of Love.

Scene 6

Narrator: Robert Crowe begins his summation by discussing the witnesses, their families, and the intense friendship between Leopold and Loeb. He appeals for the court to recall Franks's rights.

Crowe: Robert Franks had a right to live. He had a right to the society of the family and his friends, and they had a right to his society. These two young law students of superior intelligence, with more intelligence than they have heart, decided that he must die. Robert Franks was only fourteen years old.

Money is the motive in this case and I will prove it repeatedly with the defendants' own evidence. According to the psychiatrists, Loeb and Leopold discussed the idea of murder frequently. They even planned how to collect the ransom money. I used to think that the most impelling motive in life was passion, but in this case passion and a desire for revenge is swept aside for money.

Nothing, in my judgment, but an act of God is responsible for the unraveling of this terrible crime. I think that when the glasses that Leopold had not worn for three months dropped from his pocket at night, the hand of God was at work in this case. Leopold may not have believed in a God. But, if he has listened and paid attention and thought as the evidence unfolded, he must begin to believe there is a God now.

Now, I have spent more time preparing the evidence than I have in writing a closing speech. But I want to tell Your Honor that it would be much better if God had not caused this crime to be disclosed. It would be much better if it had gone unsolved, and these men had not been brought to justice. It would not have done near the harm to this community as will be done if you put your official seal of approval upon the doctrines of anarchy preached by Clarence Darrow.

Society can endure, the law can endure if criminals escape. But if a court such as this court should support the doctrines of Darrow, that you ought not to hang when the law says you should, a greater blow has been struck to our institutions than by a hundred, aye, a thousand murders.

These smart alecks are not supermen, they are not men of super intelligence. They are just a couple of spoiled smart alecks, spoiled by the petting of their folks and by the people who fawn upon them on account of their wealth.

Was this killing done, as we have been led to believe, merely for the thrill or for the excitement? The doctor reported that Loeb said he "did not anticipate the actual killing with any pleasure." It was not for the thrill or the excitement. The original crime was the kidnapping for money. The killing was an afterthought, to prevent their identification and their subsequent apprehension and punishment. He said he did not anticipate the killing with any pleasure. It was merely necessary in order to get the money.

Darrow says, "Save your sympathy for the boys. Do not place the blame on the boys. Place it on their families." Your Honor, we take boys at eighteen years of age and send them to their death in the front line trenches of France in defense of our laws. Ah, many a boy eighteen years of age, who died to defend the laws of this country, lies beneath the poppies in Flanders fields. We had no compunction when we did that. Why should we have any compunction when we take the lives of men nineteen years of age who want to tear down and destroy the laws that these brave boys died to preserve?

You have listened with a great deal of patience and kindness and consideration of the State and the defense. I am not going to trespass unduly upon Your Honor's time, and I am going to close for the State.

I believe that the facts and circumstances proved in this case demonstrate that a crime has been committed by these two defendants, and that no other punishment except the extreme penalty of the law will fit it. I leave the case with you on behalf of the State of Illinois, and I ask Your Honor in the language of the Holy Writ to "execute justice and righteousness in the land."

Note: *If preferred, suspend the script at this point to predict the outcome of the hearing.*

Scene 7

Narrator: Judge Caverly announced his decision on September 19, 1924.

John R. Caverly: The testimony introduced, both by the prosecution and the defense, has been as detailed and elaborate as though the case had been tried before a jury. By pleading guilty, the defendants have admitted legal responsibility for their acts.

The testimony in this case reveals a crime of singular atrocity. It is, in a sense, inexplicable. It was deliberately planned and prepared for during a considerable period of time. It was executed with callousness and cruelty. Under the pleas of guilty, the duty of determining the punishment for kidnapping and murder devolves upon the court, and the law indicates no rule or policy for the guidance of discretion. In choosing imprisonment instead of death, the court is moved chiefly by the consideration of the age of the defendants, boys of eighteen and nineteen years.

It is within my province to decline to impose the sentence of death on persons who are not of full age. This determination appears to be in accordance with the progress of criminal law all over the world and with the dictates of enlightened humanity. More than that, it seems to be in accordance with the precedents hitherto observed in this state. The records of Illinois show only two cases of minors who were put to death by legal process.

Life imprisonment, at the moment, strikes the public imagination as forcibly as would death by hanging; but to the offenders, particularly of the type they are, the prolonged suffering of years of confinement may well be the severest form of retribution and expiation.

The court feels it proper to add a final word concerning the effect of the parole law upon the punishment of these defendants. In the case of such atrocious crimes, it is entirely within the discretion of the department of public welfare never to grant parole. The court urges them strictly to adhere to this policy. This will both satisfy the ends of justice and safeguard the interests of society.

Narrator: Judge Caverly then passes the sentence that both Nathan Leopold and Richard Loeb are to be confined in the penitentiary at Joliet, Illinois, for the term of their natural life.

Scene 8

Narrator: Albert Loeb, who was already ill from a weak heart when the crime occurred, died a month after Richard's sentencing. Nathan Leopold's father died of heart failure a few years later, in 1929. Leopold's brothers changed their names to escape the repercussions of the scandal. Listen to other voices from that case.

Jacob Franks: I never recovered from losing Bobby—I died a few years later.

Flora Franks: I was mentally unstable throughout the trial, but I gradually recovered. Losing Jacob so soon after losing Bobby seemed uncommonly cruel. Still, I eventually remarried and tried to lead a normal life.

Richard Loeb: Nathan and I taught at the prison and did administrative work for a number of years. We were making the best of prison life. Then, on January 28, 1936, another prisoner, James Day, attacked me with a razor in the shower. I was thirty-two when I died. Cause of death? More than fifty razor wounds. Even though my throat was slashed from behind, Day claimed he had attacked me in self-defense. He didn't have a scratch on him. He was judged not guilty.

Nathan Leopold: In March of 1958, after thirty-three years in prison, I was released on parole. I went to Puerto Rico, where I went to graduate school, wrote about my life, and married. I came to the conclusion on September 15, 1963, that it all became worthwhile—that the joy of being a free man again equaled the grief of those thirty-three years. I died in 1971 at the age of sixty-six.

6

Taking the Test

The State of Tennessee vs. John Thomas Scopes
The Scopes Monkey Trial

John T. Scopes, defendant in the trial about teaching evolution. AP Photo.

INTRODUCTION

In 1925, the state of Tennessee passed House Bill 185, prohibiting the teaching of evolution in the universities and public schools. At the time, many Americans did not accept the theory of evolution, considering it to contradict the Bible. The ACLU advertised for a teacher who would agree to stand trial for teaching evolution, and town leaders of Dayton, Tennessee, decided that a trial would bring attention and commerce to their small town. John Scopes, a substitute high school teacher, agreed to become the center of a trial that is considered by many legal experts to be the trial of the century. Drawn by the legendary opposing attorneys, Clarence Darrow and William Jennings Bryan, hundreds of reporters gathered, including the famous newsman H. L. Mencken. In the first large-scale media event in U.S. history, WGN radio station from Chicago broadcast the proceedings, allowing thousands of people in the Midwest to tune in. The trial created such enduring interest that a play, *Inherit the Wind,* opened on Broadway in 1955, and a movie version followed in 1960. Because the jury actually heard little testimony, this script is expanded to include testimony, events, and conversation related to the trial.

PRESENTATION SUGGESTIONS

For Scene 1, arrange the following characters as if sitting in the drugstore: George Rappelyea, Sue Hicks (male character), Herbert Hicks, Fred "Doc" Robinson, Wallace Haggard, and John Thomas Scopes. For the remainder of the play, Judge Raulston can sit in the center of the stage, with Scopes and the team for the defense on one side of Raulston and the team for the prosecution on his other side. The narrators, witnesses, and reporters can sit on the side. Because there are so many male characters, assign roles of the narrators and the supporting attorneys to either gender. William Jennings Bryan should have a commanding voice. Clarence Darrow, who usually wore suspenders and rumpled suits, should have a folksy style. Students can research the dress of the period and prepare appropriate costumes, with the men in suits, women in short dresses. The trial took place in July in a stifling courtroom.

RELATED BOOKS

Blake, Arthur. *The Scopes Trial: Defending the Right to Teach.* Brookfield, CT: Millbrook Press, 1994.

Caudill, Edward. *The Scopes Trial: A Photographic History.* Knoxville, TN: The University of Tennessee Press, 2000.

CHARACTERS

Narrator 1

George Rappelyea, *Dayton businessman*

Sue Hicks, *Dayton attorney and Herbert's brother*

Herbert Hicks, *Dayton attorney and Sue's brother*

Fred "Doc" Robinson, *owner of Robinson's Drugstore and chairman of the school board*

Wallace Haggard, *Dayton attorney*

Narrator 2

John Thomas Scopes, *high school biology teacher*

Charles, *reporter*

Henry, *reporter*

John T. Raulston, *judge*

John Neal, *dean of the School of Law at the University of Tennessee and defense attorney*

A. Thomas Stewart, *attorney general for the 18th Judicial Court and prosecuting attorney*

Clarence Darrow, *reknowned defense attorney*

Arthur Garfield Hays, *ACLU lawyer*

Benjamin G. McKenzie, *prosecuting attorney*

Dudley Field Malone, *defense attorney*

Howard Morgan, *student*

Maynard M. Metcalf, *professor of zoology from Johns Hopkins University*

William Jennings Bryan, *prosecuting attorney*

Taking the Test

The State of Tennessee vs. John Thomas Scopes
The Scopes Monkey Trial

Scene 1

Narrator 1: On the morning of May 5, 1925, five men are enjoying a break from the heat over soft drinks at Robinson's Drug Store in Dayton, Tennessee. George Rappelyea, a civil engineer, had noticed an ad in the *Chattanooga Daily News* placed by the American Civil Liberties Union. The ACLU, founded in 1920 to protect the civil rights of people, was asking for a teacher to voluntarily admit to teaching evolution. The ACLU hopes to demonstrate the unconstitutionality of the Butler Act, which prohibits the teaching of the evolution theory in all public schools in the state of Tennessee.

George Rappelyea: My friends, look at this ad. The ACLU is willing to pay all expenses to any teacher willing to go on trial for teaching evolution. You know, that Butler Act makes it illegal to teach evolution in a public school. I believe in the teachings of the Bible, but I also believe in evolution.

Sue Hicks: Maybe we should try to find a volunteer here in Dayton. Come to think of it, if we could get that trial here, it would serve two purposes—test the constitutionality of the law and put Dayton on the map.

Herbert Hicks: Doc, you're chairman of the school board. Who teaches biology at the high school?

Fred "Doc" Robinson: William Ferguson, but he has a wife and children. But . . . John Scopes, the football coach, has been substituting for him in the biology class. He's single and seems levelheaded. Maybe he'd be willing.

Wallace Haggard: Let's get him here and see what he thinks.

Narrator 2: While a boy finds Scopes, who is playing tennis, the men look at a copy of Hunter's *Civic Biology,* written by George William Hunter and sold by Doc Robinson in his store. Scopes arrives from his game and joins the men.

George Rappelyea: John, we've been talking. Do you agree that nobody could teach biology without teaching evolution?

John Thomas Scopes: Of course.

Sue Hicks: Have you been teaching evolution?

John Thomas Scopes: I only helped the students review for the year-end tests.

Wallace Haggard: Did that include evolution at all? Can you show us where evolution is taught in the textbook?

John Thomas Scopes: You can see in these diagrams that man is shown to be descended from other animals. I did teach from the book, so I suppose you could say I've been teaching evolution.

Fred "Doc" Robinson: Then you've been violating the law. The Butler Act states that it's unlawful for any teacher in public schools to teach any theory that denies the story of the creation of man as taught in the Bible.

John Thomas Scopes: I never thought about that. I was just teaching biology from the textbook.

Fred "Doc" Robinson: Take a look at this ad. The ACLU is looking for a teacher who would test the constitutionality of the Butler Act. Would you volunteer to go on record as having taught evolution?

Herbert Hicks: It could be important to education and to Dayton. The most that would happen is that you'd be fined and have to pay court costs. It appears the ACLU will cover that.

John Thomas Scopes: If I can qualify as a defendant, then I'll be willing to stand trial.

Fred "Doc" Robinson: That's good enough for me. I'm going to call the newspaper right now and let them know we've arrested a man for teaching evolution.

Scene 2

Narrator 1: Much of the controversy about evolution comes from a book entitled *On the Origin of Species by Means of Natural Selection,* published in 1859 by English naturalist Charles Darwin. Darwin described his theory that all animals are descended from a common ancestor. His theory also held that the organisms best suited or most adaptable to a place and climate survived while those least fit died off. This is referred to as the "survival of the fittest" or "natural selection."

Narrator 2: Darwin's theories collide with the beliefs of fundamentalists, the term given to people who believe in the literal truth of the Bible. Darwin's theories, for example, seem to contradict the notions that God created man in His image in one day and all the animals in two days.

Narrator 1: The ACLU asserts that the Butler Act, passed in Tennessee on March 21, 1925, violates the U.S. Constitution, which provides for the separation of church and state and allows for free speech. The ACLU hopes that the case will wind up in the State Supreme Court—and that the law will be overturned. With Scopes's agreement to admit to teaching evolution, the ACLU has its test case.

Narrator 2: Trials are held quickly in the 1920s. By July 7, Dayton has begun to swell with peddlers selling Bibles alongside buttons that say "Your Old Man's a Monkey." Two of the more than 200 reporters in Dayton for the trial discuss the key attorneys for both sides.

Charles: I wouldn't have missed this for the world, Henry. Imagine being able to hear two of the best attorneys in the land fight this one out.

Henry: You're right, Charles. It's hard to imagine two better opponents than William Jennings Bryan and Clarence Darrow. I've heard Bryan speak several times when he ran for president. Hard to believe he lost his bid for the presidency three times—he is one powerful speaker.

Charles: I read that he can be heard speaking from a quarter mile away—do you think that's true?

Henry: I believe it. He's about as famous for speeches against evolution as he is for his politics. He just seems perfect for proving that Scopes broke the law when he taught biology.

Charles: But what about Darrow? He has a much different style, but he managed to keep Nathan Leopold and Richard Loeb from being executed for killing that fourteen-year-old boy in Chicago.

Henry: Darrow is brilliant, I'll grant that. So who do you think will win?

Charles: No question. Bryan will win. After all, Scopes taught from a textbook that has evolution in it. He's even admitted to it!

Henry: But that book is used all over the country.

Charles: But the point is—teaching evolution is against the law in Tennessee.

Henry: Well, it's going to be interesting to see how this plays out. Did you hear that WGN radio from Chicago will be broadcasting the trial?

Charles: Imagine that! Who would think that the public would be that interested in a trial?

Scene 3

Narrator 1: In addition to Bryan, other members of the prosecution include his son, William Jennings, Jr., the Hicks brothers, Sue and Herbert, Wallace Haggard, Benjamin G. McKenzie and his son J. Gordon McKenzie, and A. Thomas Stewart, the attorney general for the 18th Judicial Court.

Narrator 2: Joining Clarence Darrow are Arthur Garfield Hays of the ACLU, John Neal, who is dean of the School of Law at the University of Tennessee, Neal's associate, F. B. McElwee, and Dudley Field Malone. Malone had served as assistant secretary of state when Bryan was secretary of state from 1913–1915 under President Woodrow Wilson.

THE STATE OF TENNESSEE VS. JOHN THOMAS SCOPES

Narrator 1: On a hot Friday, July 7, Judge John T. Raulston allows 900 people to squeeze into a courtroom designed to hold 700. Previously, on May 25, a grand jury had determined that the state had cause to try Scopes. Now, concerned that procedures had not been followed, the grand jury convenes again, and the process is repeated. Once again, a grand jury finds just cause to accuse Scopes of breaking a state law, and the jury selection begins. By the end of the day, the jury is chosen and the judge adjourns the proceedings until Monday morning.

Narrator 2: On Monday, as scheduled, the indictment is read into the record. Judge Raulston turns to the defense team.

John T. Raulston: What is your plea, gentlemen?

John Neal: May it please Your Honor, we make a motion to quash the indictment. The Butler Act violates ten different articles of the constitution of Tennessee. For example, the Tennessee Constitution provides that no preference shall ever be given, by law, to any religious establishment or mode of worship. Further, the Butler Act violates the U.S. Constitution—specifically the right of freedom of speech. The free communication of thoughts and opinions is one of the invaluable rights of man, and every citizen may freely speak, write, and print on any subject.

A. Thomas Stewart: Your Honor, these arguments do not concern the jury. They are limited to the nature of the law. The jury could be prejudiced by hearing the arguments. They should leave the courtroom.

Clarence Darrow: I object to removing the jury.

Narrator 1: Darrow reasons that the jury will only benefit from hearing the argument about whether the law is wrong, but the judge agrees with Stewart and sends the jury out. After Neal concludes his arguments, Arthur Garfield Hays, the ACLU lawyer, adds his arguments.

Arthur Garfield Hays: If a law against teaching about evolution is constitutional, then so would be a law—let's call it the Hays Act—against teaching about the solar system. It would be unlawful to teach any theory that denies the story that the earth is the center of the universe, as taught in the Bible, and to teach instead that the earth and planets move around the sun. With the Hays Act, just as the Italian philosopher Giordano Bruno was burned at the stake in 1600 for teaching that the earth and planets move around the sun, any teacher found guilty of teaching such information should be put to death.

Narrator 2: The arguments continue, with Attorney General Stewart responding to the arguments after the midday recess.

A. Thomas Stewart: Let's start with the assertion that the Butler Act interferes with religious worship. Why, students can attend the public schools of this state and go to any church they please. The Butler Act doesn't interfere with freedom of speech either. Mr. Scopes might have taken his stand on the street corners and expounded until he became hoarse and we could not interfere with him. But he cannot go into the public schools and *teach* this theory.

Narrator 1: The defense always has the last word when a motion is under consideration. The audience becomes quiet and attentive when Clarence Darrow stands, hooks his thumbs under his suspenders, and begins to talk in a folksy manner.

Clarence Darrow: If today you can take a thing like evolution and make it a crime to teach it in the public school, tomorrow you can make it a crime to teach it in the private schools, and the next year you can make it a crime to teach it in the church. At the next session you may ban books and the newspapers. Soon, you may set Catholic against Protestant and Protestant against Protestant, and try to foist your own religion upon the minds of men. If you can do one, you can do the other. Ignorance and fanaticism is ever busy and needs feeding. Today, it is the public school teachers; tomorrow, the private. The next day, the preachers and the lectures, the magazines, the books, the newspapers. After a while, Your Honor, it is the setting of man against man and creed against creed until with flying banners and beating drums, we are marching backward to the glorious ages of the sixteenth century when bigots lighted torches to burn the men who dared to bring any intelligence and enlightenment and culture to the human mind.

John T. Raulston: I shall take your arguments under advisement and read my decision in the morning. The court is adjourned.

Scene 4

Narrator 2: The next morning the bailiff calls the courtroom to order, and Judge Raulston follows the usual tradition for beginning the day.

John T. Raulston: Reverend Stribling, will you open with prayer?

Clarence Darrow: I object to prayer and I object to the jury being present when the court rules on the objection.

A. Thomas Stewart: But the jury is not here.

John T. Raulston: I do not want to be unreasonable about anything, but I believe I am responsible for the conduct of the court. It has been my custom to have prayers in the courtroom when it was convenient. I know of no reason why I should not follow up this custom, so I will overrule the objection.

Narrator 2: Darrow does not let the issue rest.

Clarence Darrow: We took no exceptions on the first day, but this has persisted in every session. The nature of this case involves the state claiming that there is a conflict between science and religion. Above all other cases there should be no attempt by means of prayer or in any other way to influence the deliberation of the jury in the facts in this case.

Benjamin G. McKenzie: Our supreme court has ruled on this matter. Juries may ask for divine guidance.

Clarence Darrow: I do not object to the jury or anyone else praying in secret or in private.

But I do object to turning this courtroom into a meetinghouse in this case. You have no right to do it.

Narrator 1: The attorneys debate the issue, with Stewart labeling Darrow an agnostic, one who believes that it is impossible to know if God exists. He emphasizes that Darrow, having come from another part of the country, doesn't know the thoughts of the local people. Dudley Malone rises to Darrow's defense.

Dudley Field Malone: As one of the members of counsel who is not an agnostic, I would like to state my objection. Your Honor has the discretion to have a prayer or not to have a prayer. There was no exception felt to the prayer the first day. But has Your Honor had a clergyman open every trial every morning of every day with prayer? We believe that the daily prayers help increase the atmosphere of hostility to our point of view, which already exists in this community.

A. Thomas Stewart: I would advise Mr. Malone that this is a God-fearing country.

Dudley Field Malone: It is no more a God-fearing country than that from which I came.

John T. Raulston: Gentleman, do not turn this into an argument. In the years I have been on the bench, I have used my discretion in opening the court with prayer. I see nothing that might influence the court or jury as to the issues. I believe in prayer myself. I invoke divine guidance myself, when I am on the bench and off the bench. I see no reason why I should not continue to do this. The objection is overruled.

Narrator 2: Judge Raulston explains that the power failure of the previous night prevented him from finishing his written ruling on the motion to quash the indictment. The court is adjourned until the following morning to give him time to write his ruling.

Scene 5

Narrator 1: The fourth day of the trial opens with Raulston reading into the record his opinion on the motion to Neal's arguments requesting the judge to quash the indictment. To no one's surprise, Raulston overrules the motion, and Scopes's plea of not guilty is entered into the record.

Narrator 2: Meanwhile, the reporters, Charles and Henry, chat quietly in the back of the courtroom.

Charles: Seems to me that this case is about over. Everyone knows that Scopes is guilty.

Henry: It won't last long. No one wants Scopes to be cleared, including the ACLU.

Charles: I don't get it. Why did they send Darrow and all the other attorneys?

Henry: I think it's just for show. They need to make it look good and put on a strong defense. Then they can appeal the case to a higher court. That's when it will count—especially if the state supreme court overturns the ruling. No one really cares what happens at the county level. First they have to lose, so it will be appealed—but it has to look good.

Charles: You've got a point, Henry. You're probably right.

Narrator 1: After the foreman of the jury requests fans for the hot courtroom, the prosecution makes a brief opening statement.

A. Thomas Stewart: It is the insistence of the State that John Thomas Scopes has violated the antievolution law by teaching the theory that man is descended from animals. Therefore, he has taught a theory that denies the story of divine creation of man as taught by the Bible.

Narrator 2: As Henry suspected, it now becomes clear that the defense will be a strong one.

Dudley Field Malone: The purpose of the defense will be to set before you all available facts and information from science to aid you in forming an opinion of what evolution is. The defense denies that it is part of any movement or conspiracy on the part of scientists to destroy the authority of Christianity or the Bible. The narrow purpose of the defense is to establish the innocence of the defendant, Mr. Scopes. The broad purpose of the defense will be to prove that the Bible is a work of religious aspiration and rules of conduct that must be kept in the field of theology. We maintain that science and religion embrace two separate and distinct fields of thought and learning. We will also show that there are millions of people who believe in evolution and in the stories of creation as set forth in the Bible and who find no conflict between the two. The defense maintains that there is a clear distinction between God, the church, the Bible, Christianity—and Mr. Bryan!

Narrator 1: After a few good-natured exchanges, the jury is finally sworn. The prosecution calls its first witness, Walter White, the superintendent of schools, who testifies that John Scopes admitted to teaching about evolution. Next, Howard Morgan, a student, takes the stand.

A. Thomas Stewart: Your name is Howard Morgan?

Howard Morgan: Yes, sir.

A. Thomas Stewart: Did you study this science book with Professor Scopes?

Howard Morgan: Yes, sir.

A. Thomas Stewart: Now, how did Professor Scopes teach that book to you? I mean by that, did he ask you questions and you answered them or did he give you lectures, or both?

Howard Morgan: Well, sometimes he would ask us questions and then he would lecture to us on different subjects in the book.

A. Thomas Stewart: Did he ever teach you anything about evolution?

Howard Morgan: Yes, sir. He said that the earth was once a hot molten mass too hot for plant or animal life to exist upon it. In the sea, the earth cooled off. There was a little germ of one-cell organism formed, and this organism kept evolving until it got to be a land animal and it kept on evolving. From this it became man.

A. Thomas Stewart: How did he classify man with reference to other animals?

Howard Morgan: The book and he both classified man along with cats and dogs, cows, horses, monkeys, lions, horses, and all that.

A. Thomas Stewart: What did he say they were?

Howard Morgan: Mammals.

Narrator 2: Clarence Darrow conducts the cross-examination.

Clarence Darrow: Howard, what do you mean by classify?

Howard Morgan: Well, it means classify these animals we mentioned, that men were just the same as them, in other words . . .

Clarence Darrow: He didn't say a cat was the same as a man?

Howard Morgan: No, sir. He said man had a reasoning power—that these animals did not.

Clarence Darrow: *(laughing)* There is some doubt about that.

Narrator 1: The courtroom erupts in laughter as Judge Raulston calls for order. After a few more questions about Scopes's teachings, Darrow asks a final question.

Clarence Darrow: Now, Professor Scopes's teaching—it hasn't hurt you any, has it?

Howard Morgan: No, sir.

Clarence Darrow: That's all.

Scene 6

Narrator 2: The case for the defense rests on expert testimony, and the defense opens by calling Maynard M. Metcalf, a professor of zoology from Johns Hopkins University. Before he begins to testify, Stewart raises an issue.

A. Thomas Stewart: Your Honor, Tennessee requires a defendant to take the stand first or not at all.

Clarence Darrow: Your Honor, every single word said against this defendant was true.

John T. Raulston: So he does not care to go on the stand?

Clarence Darrow: What is the use?

John T. Raulston: Then continue with your witness.

Clarence Darrow: Professor Metcalf, are you an evolutionist?

Maynard M. Metcalf: Surely.

Clarence Darrow: Do you know any scientific man in the world who is not an evolutionist?

A. Thomas Stewart: We object to that. Further, we object to the jury being here to listen to this discussion as to the admissibility of expert testimony.

Narrator 1: After some discussion, the judge dismisses the jury again, reminding them that they are not to listen to the radio news reports being broadcast on loudspeakers outside the courtroom.

John T. Raulston: Before I can rule on the admissibility of the testimony, I need to know more. Please continue.

Maynard M. Metcalf: Evolution and the theories of evolution are two different things. Scientists agree that evolution occurred, but not about how. There are dozens of theories of evolution, some of which are almost wholly absurd. Some are largely mistaken, and some are perhaps almost wholly true.

Clarence Darrow: How long ago did life begin on earth?

Maynard M. Metcalf: I would have to answer based on what I have heard from others.

Clarence Darrow: More than 6,000 years ago, wasn't it?

Narrator 2: Darrow is referring to the belief by fundamentalists that man was created in approximately 4000 B.C.

Maynard M. Metcalf: Well, 600 million years ago is a modest guess.

Clarence Darrow: And you say that evolution, as you speak of it, includes man?

Maynard M. Metcalf: Surely.

Narrator 1: The court adjourns for the evening. The next morning, arguments regarding the admissibility of admitting expert testimony resume. The jury is still excluded from the courtroom. After attorneys for both sides have presented arguments, the audience is pleased when William Jennings Bryan rises to speak.

William Jennings Bryan: This is not the place to try to prove that the law ought never to have been passed. The place to prove that, or teach that, was the legislature. It isn't proper to bring experts in here to try to defeat the purpose of the people of this state by trying to show that this thing that they denounce and outlaw is a beautiful thing that everybody ought to believe in. Let's look at this another way. Let's suppose a man made a contract with somebody to bring rain here in a dry season. Let's say he was to get $500 for each inch of rain. If the rain did not come, and he sued to enforce his contract and collect the money, could he bring in experts to prove that a drought was better than a rain?

Narrator 2: After the laughter subsides, Bryan holds up a copy of Hunter's *Civic Biology* and continues to use humor as he ridicules the text, especially the fact that man is in a small circle with other mammals.

William Jennings Bryan: This is the book where they were teaching your children that man was a mammal, and so indistinguishable among mammals that they leave him there with 3,499 other mammals—including elephants! Talk about putting Daniel in the lion's den! How dare those scientists put man in a little ring like that with lions and tigers and everything that is bad. . . . The facts are simple. The case is plain. And if those gentlemen want to enter upon a larger field of educational work on the subject of evolution, let them get through with this case and then convene a mock court. For it would deserve the title of mock court if its purpose is to banish from the hearts of the people the word of God as revealed!

Narrator 1: The courtroom erupts in applause. But Bryan is not to have the last word. Dudley Field Malone, Bryan's former assistant, rises to respond. Malone is one of the few men who has kept on his jacket in the stifling courtroom. Now he quietly removes his jacket, folds it neatly, and lays it on the defense counsel's table.

Dudley Field Malone: *(wearily)* Whether Mr. Bryan knows it or not, he is a mammal, he is an animal, and he is man. Are we to have our children know nothing about science except what the church says they shall know? I have never seen harm in learning and understanding, in humility and open-mindedness. And I have never seen clearer the need of that learning than when I see the attitude of the prosecution, who attack and refuse to accept the information and intelligence that expert witnesses will give them.

Narrator 2: The audience is drawn in by Malone's mounting passion and his eloquence.

Malone: There is never a duel with truth. The truth always wins and we are not afraid of it. The truth does not need the law. The truth does not need the force of government. The truth does not need Mr. Bryan. The truth is eternal and immortal. We are ready to tell the truth as we understand it and we do not fear all the truth that they can present as facts. We are ready. We feel we stand with progress . . . with science . . . with intelligence . . . with fundamental freedom in America. We are not afraid. Where is the fear? We meet it. Where is the fear? We defy it. We ask Your Honor to admit the evidence as a matter of correct law, as a matter of sound procedure, and as a matter of justice to the defense in this case.

Narrator 1: Once again, the courtroom erupts in applause that the judge cannot stop. The people came to hear William Jennings Bryan, but they have been captivated by Dudley Field Malone. When the court finally adjourns, Bryan, Scopes, and Malone remain sitting at their tables.

William Jennings Bryan: *(quietly)* Dudley, that was the greatest speech I have ever heard.

Dudley Field Malone: Thank you, Mr. Bryan—I am sorry it was I who had to make it.

Scene 7

Narrator 2: Friday morning, no one is surprised when the judge opens the proceedings by sustaining the motion to exclude expert testimony. Judge Raulston does agree to allowing the attorneys to read into the record what the experts would have said. The jury won't get to hear the experts, but the information will be on record for an appeal to a higher court.

Narrator 1: When the judge refuses Darrow's request to have time to write the testimony, tempers flare.

Clarence Darrow: If Your Honor takes a half day to write an opinion—

John T. Raulston: I have not taken—

Clarence Darrow: We want to make statements here that we expect to prove. I do not understand why every request of the State is given considerable time and discussion, and any suggestion on our part is immediately overruled.

John T. Raulston: I hope you don't mean to reflect on the integrity of the court?

Clarence Darrow: *(drily)* Well, Your Honor has the right to hope.

John T. Raulston: I have the right to do something else, perhaps!

Clarence Darrow: All right. All right.

Narrator 2: Darrow smiles as he turns away. Judge Raulston, who is extremely angry, abruptly adjourns court until Monday morning. Darrow now has time to prepare his experts' written statements and read them into the record.

Narrator 1: Once again, the jury has missed everything of interest. Henry and Charles discuss the new developments.

Henry: Say, Charles, what do you think will happen on Monday?

Charles: I think the case is pretty much over. Darrow can't have much more to say—he's lost the case anyway. I told you when this started that Bryan was going to win. I think I'm going to pack up and head home.

Henry: I don't know, Henry. Raulston was pretty angry when he adjourned. I think he might find Darrow in contempt.

Charles: Well, that would liven things up a bit. Maybe I'll stay around.

Narrator 2: As Henry suspected, Raulston has decided over the weekend to cite Darrow for contempt. Monday opens with Raulston's statements.

John T. Raulston: It has been my policy on the bench to be cautious and avoid rushing to conclusions. But in the face of what I consider an unjustified expression of contempt for this court by Clarence Darrow, I am impelled to call upon Darrow and ask why he should not be dealt with for contempt. I hereby order that he be required to appear in this court at nine o'clock, Tuesday, July 21, 1925, and answer this citation. The bond will be $5,000.

Narrator 1: The morning proceeds with the reading of the expert testimony about evolution and the Bible into the record, with the jury excluded as usual. After lunch, the judge agrees to allow Darrow to speak. After a lengthy statement of apology, Darrow wraps up.

Clarence Darrow: Your Honor, I went further than I should have. I had not the slightest thought to insult the court. I don't know as I was ever in a community in my life where my religious ideas differed as widely from the great mass as since I've been in Tennessee. I came here a perfect stranger and I have not found discourtesy from any citizen. I have been treated better, kindlier, and more hospitably than I fancied I would. I am quite certain that the remark should not have been made. I am sorry and I want to apologize to the court.

John T. Raulston: When a judge speaks from the bench, his acts are not personal but are part of the machine that is part of the great state where he lives. I could not afford to pass those words by without notice. The Man that I believe came into the world to save man from sin, the Man that died on the cross that man might be redeemed, taught that it was godly to forgive. I believe in Christ. I believe in these principles. I accept Colonel Darrow's apology.

Narrator 2: The men shake hands and the trial proceeds.

Scene 8

Narrator 1: The jury is brought in, and Hays calls William Jennings Bryan to the stand as an expert witness on the Bible.

John T. Raulston: *(weakly)* Do you think you have a right—

Narrator 2: When it becomes clear that Bryan welcomes the chance to testify, reserving the right to call the defense attorneys as well, the judge allows Bryan to take the stand.

Clarence Darrow: You have given considerable study to the Bible, haven't you, Mr. Bryan?

William Jennings Bryan: Yes, sir, I have tried to.

Clarence Darrow: You claim that everything in the Bible should be literally interpreted?

William Jennings Bryan: I believe everything in the Bible should be accepted as it is given there. Some of the Bible is given illustratively. For instance, *Ye are the salt of the earth.* I would not insist that man was actually salt.

Clarence Darrow: The Bible says Joshua commanded the sun to stand still for the purpose of lengthening the day, and you believe it.

William Jennings Bryan: I do.

Clarence Darrow: Mr. Bryan, have you pondered what would happen if the earth stood still suddenly?

William Jennings Bryan: No.

Clarence Darrow: Do you believe that the sun went around the earth?

William Jennings Bryan: No, I believe that the earth goes around the sun.

Clarence Darrow: Do you think the earth was made in six days?

William Jennings Bryan: Not days of twenty-four hours. My impression is that they were periods, but I would not attempt to argue against anybody who wanted to believe in literal days.

Clarence Darrow: Do you believe that the first woman was Eve?

William Jennings Bryan: I do.

Clarence Darrow: Do you believe she was literally made out of Adam's rib?

William Jennings Bryan: I do.

Narrator 1: Darrow continues his intense questioning on points of the Bible until Bryan loses patience.

William Jennings Bryan: Your Honor, I think I can shorten this testimony. The only purpose Mr. Darrow has is to slur at the Bible. I want the world to know that this man, who does not believe in a God, is trying to use a court in Tennessee to slur at it. While it will require time, I am willing to take it.

Clarence Darrow: I object to your statement. I am examining you on your fool ideas that no intelligent Christian on earth believes!

John T. Raulston: The time is late. Court is adjourned until nine o'clock tomorrow morning.

Scene 9

Narrator 2: On Tuesday, the eighth day of the trial, everyone is back in the courtroom. Bryan and Darrow are ready to continue their duel of words. Bryan is ready to examine Darrow and the other defense attorneys. The judge surprises the court with other plans.

John T. Raulston: I feel that the testimony of Mr. Bryan can shed no light on any issues that will be pending before the higher courts. I am going to expunge Mr. Bryan's testimony from yesterday, and it will not be considered.

Narrator 1: With this change in plans, there is little left for Darrow to say. The judge meets privately with the attorneys and they agree to conclude the trial. The jurors are brought in and Raulston prepares them for closing arguments, with one important instruction included in his comments.

John T. Raulston: The court charges you that, in order to prove its case, the State does not have to specifically prove that the defendant taught a theory that denied the story of the divine creation of man as taught in the Bible, other than to prove that he taught that man descended from a lower order of animals.

Narrator 2: Darrow then addresses the jury, essentially telling them to convict John Scopes.

Clarence Darrow: The court has told you very plainly that if you think my client taught that man descended from a lower order of animals, you will find him guilty. You heard the testimony and there is no dispute of the facts. Scopes did not go on the stand because he could not deny the statements made by his students. This law will never be decided until it gets to a higher court, and it cannot get to a higher court unless you bring in a verdict. I guess that is plain enough.

Narrator 1: And now, you the audience must weigh the facts as you have heard them. Should John Scopes be convicted?

Scene 10

Narrator 2: The jury deliberates for nine minutes, finding the defendant guilty, but they leave the determination of the fine to the judge. Raulston sets the fine at $100 and asks Scopes if he has anything to say.

John Thomas Scopes: Your Honor, I feel that I have been convicted of violating an unjust statute. I will continue in the future, as I have in the past, to oppose this law in any way I can. Any other action would be in violation of my ideal of academic freedom—that is, to teach the truth as guaranteed in our Constitution of personal and religious freedom. I think the fine is unjust.

Narrator 1: The attorneys make farewell addresses, and Judge Raulston concludes by having a local pastor pronounce a benediction.

Narrator 2: The Sunday after the trial, Bryan attends the local church, has dinner, and takes a nap from which he never awakens. Bryan, who had diabetes, suffers a stroke and dies in his sleep.

Narrator 1: In June 1926, Darrow argues the case before the Tennessee supreme court in Nashville. The justices take the case under advisement and announce their opinion on January 14, 1928, stating that the Butler Act is constitutional. However, they rule that any fine in excess of $50 should have been determined by the jury, not by Judge Raulston. The five justices overturn Scopes's conviction on a technicality.

Narrator 2: The Butler Act remains in effect until it is repealed by the State of Tennessee in 1967.

7

An Arrogant Man

The Trial of David C. Stephenson,
Grand Dragon of the Ku Klux Klan

David C. Stephenson, former Ku Klux Klan Dragon and defendant in the murder of Madge Oberholtzer. Bettmann/CORBIS.

INTRODUCTION

The Ku Klux Klan, a white supremacist organization created in 1866 by Confederate Civil War veterans, had evolved into a powerful force by the 1920s. Membership was especially strong in the Midwest, with up to ten percent of the population of Indiana belonging. Because many people were worried about immigration, blacks, Jews, and Catholics (and even feared that the Vatican would be moved to the United States), membership grew quickly. New recruits paid a ten-dollar "klecktoken" to join. Four dollars went to the person, called a *kleagle,* who brought in the new member. Another dollar went to the king kleagle, fifty cents to the local grand goblin, with the balance mailed to the national office in Atlanta (Lutholtz, 29). So a charismatic leader could become wealthy through the Klan. David C. Stephenson was just that leader, prompting unprecedented increases in enrollment while integrating himself in the political power structures in Indiana. However, his tenure as Grand Dragon was short lived, due to his conviction for the murder of Madge Oberholtzer, a young woman who had been assisting him with various projects. The scandal of the trial and its aftermath ruined Stephenson's career and prompted the decline of the Klan in Indiana. Within a year of Stephenson's conviction, Klan membership dropped to 15,000 (Grant and Katz, 142).

Note: Because the trial involves a graphic discussion of Miss Oberholtzer's assault, preread the script to determine if this material is appropriate for your class.

PRESENTATION SUGGESTIONS

Arrange the characters in three tiers. Have the narrators, D. C. Stephenson, Hiram and Mrs. Evans, Madge Oberholtzer, and Mrs. Oberholtzer sit on the top tier. Place Asa J. Smith, Eunice Schultz, Dr. Kingsbury, Dr. Moon, Cora Householder, and Dr. Ailstock in the middle tier. Have the attorneys sit on the bottom tier. Women of this period often wore mid-calf length suits, short skirts, or dresses with dropped hemlines and had "bobbed" hair. See examples at http://www.rambova.com/fashion/ fash4.html. Men often wore fedoras and pin-striped suits, with pants tapered at the ankles.

RELATED BOOKS AND WEB SITE

Grant, Robert, and Joseph Katz. *The Great Trials of the Twenties: The Watershed Decade in America's Courtrooms.* Rockville Centre, NY: Sarpedon, 1998.

Lutholtz, William M. *Grand Dragon: D. C. Stephenson and the Ku Klux Klan in Indiana.* West Lafayette, IN: Purdue University Press, 1991.

http://www.statelib.lib.in.us/ www/isl/indiana/Klan.html

THE TRIAL OF DAVID C. STEPHENSON

CHARACTERS

Narrator 1

Narrator 2

D. C. Stephenson, *Grand Dragon of the KKK*

Hiram Evans, *Imperial Wizard of the KKK*

Mrs. Evans, *Hiram's wife*

Mrs. Oberholtzer, *Madge Oberholtzer's mother*

Madge Oberholtzer, *Stephenson's former assistant and deceased victim of assault*

Asa J. Smith, *attorney and friend of the Oberholtzer family*

Eunice Schultz, *boarder at the Oberholtzer home*

Dr. Kingsbury, *Oberholtzer physician*

Charles Cox, *prosecuting attorney*

Will Remy, *prosecuting attorney*

Dr. Moon, *pathologist*

Ira Holmes, *defense attorney*

Cora Householder, *neighbor to the Oberholtzers and surprise witness*

Dr. Ailstock, *dentist and friend of Stephenson*

Floyd Christian, *defense attorney*

Ephraim Inman, *defense attorney*

An Arrogant Man

The Trial of David C. Stephenson Grand Dragon of the Ku Klux Klan

Scene 1

Narrator 1: On July 4, 1923, in Kokomo, Indiana, an estimated 50,000 members of the Ku Klux Klan watch the skies expectantly. Each Klansman is anxious to see and hear their next Grand Dragon—David Curtis Stephenson.

Narrator 2: Members of the Klan, committed to preserving white supremacy, not only fear the influx of blacks in the north, they also worry about the growing influences of Catholics, Jews, immigrants, and foreigners. The members dedicate themselves to ensuring that a white, Protestant America reigns supreme.

Narrator 1: One Klansman has emerged as a powerful force in Indiana. That man is David Curtis Stephenson. As the Klansmen watch, a small plane lands and a large man climbs to the ground. Stephenson greets the robed and hooded Klansmen as his inauguration as Grand Dragon begins.

D. C. Stephenson: My worthy subjects, citizens of the Invisible Empire, Klansmen all, greetings. It grieves me to be late. The President of the United States kept me unduly long, counseling upon vital matters of state. Only my pleas that this is the time and place of my coronation obtained for me surcease from his prayers for guidance.

Narrator 2: Stephenson's subsequent speech on "100 Percent Americanism" excites the crowd. The Imperial Wizard Hiram Evans then addresses the crowd.

Hiram Evans: I am proud to be in this great state to see the amazing growth of the Klan in Indiana. On this great day I am awarding ninety-two official charters! And this man standing in front of you is responsible for our tremendous success. And now I would like the Old Man to return to the stage for his inauguration.

Narrator 1: At age thirty-one, Stephenson is not an old man, but the laws of the Klan forbid speaking his name aloud. Even the reporters in the crowd have sworn not to reveal Stephenson's name in print. After being presented with the golden-orange robe and hood of the Grand Dragon's office, a gold medallion, and a jeweled cross, Stephenson again addresses the crowd.

D. C. Stephenson: My friends, I want to talk to you about a bit of history, those people who made our country the fine place that it is today—and the place that we are sworn to protect. I am talking about such greats as Benjamin Franklin and Thomas Jefferson. I have studied the minds and motives of these constitutional builders. I want to bring them here and let them talk to you, through my humble interpretation, about their creation in its relations to our government and our public problems as they exist today. If the founding fathers were here today, they would support the changes I am going to propose. *(pausing)* Let's start with inflation. If inflation is not controlled, the middle class will be wiped out.

Narrator 2: Stephenson goes on to propose sweeping changes, many of which appeal to the listeners. Later, Stephenson leaves with his bodyguards, and the crowd prepares for an evening parade and fireworks. The day ends with great pageantry.

Scene 2

Narrator 1: Later, Stephenson buys a home in Irvington, Indiana. His Klan activities and increasing power have made him very wealthy. He enjoys his life—the money, the power, and the women. Although Imperial Wizard Hiram Evans appreciates Stephenson's success, there is tension between the two men. He begins to have doubts about his activities. Evans discusses his concerns with his wife.

Hiram Evans: I really don't know what to make of Stephenson sometimes.

Mrs. Evans: What's troubling you about him?

Hiram Evans: He's done a great job of recruiting members. And he's turned back his salary so it can be used to further our cause.

Mrs. Evans: It sounds like he's very devoted. What could be wrong about that?

Hiram Evans: It just doesn't make sense. He gets more and more wealthy. He spent more than $20,000 renovating his new home. It looks just like the headquarters in Atlanta now.

Mrs. Evans: What about having his books audited?

Hiram Evans: I already did that and the accountants didn't find anything. Yet he's bought several new cars and a yacht. And there are other things that bother me about him.

Mrs. Evans: What sort of things?

Hiram Evans: All these rumors about women. He seems to get engaged every few months.

Mrs. Evans: Maybe he's just having a hard time settling down. He's still young, and he does seem to work very hard.

Hiram Evans: Yes . . . but I just wish I could trust him. I haven't any choice except to continue to monitor him closely. There's too much at stake, including my own future in the Klan.

Narrator 2: Evans does keep up the pressure on Stephenson, and the tension proves stressful. Even though Stephenson has been Grand Dragon just a few months, he begins to consider retiring from his position. However, by November 1923, the two men strike an uneasy truce—for the good of the Klan.

Scene 3

Narrator 1: By 1925, Stephenson's control extends to the governor and several legislators. His interests are diverse, including even developing a nutrition textbook that would be used in all the Indiana schools. This would become one of many lucrative ventures for Stephenson, having purchased the publishing company that would publish the book.

Narrator 2: On the evening of March 15, 1925, Madge Oberholtzer, a young woman who was hired to help Stephenson on the textbook and other projects, has arrived home from a Sunday drive. It's nearly 10 P.M.

Mrs. Oberholtzer: Madge, you have a message from Mr. Stephenson. I think he needs to talk to you about the nutrition book. He'd like you to call.

Madge Oberholtzer: Alright, Mother.

Narrator 1: Madge calls and learns that Stephenson wants to see her before he leaves for Chicago. She bids good night to her mother.

Madge Oberholtzer: Mother, Mr. Stephenson is sending one of his men to get me so we can meet tonight.

Mrs. Oberholtzer: So late?

Madge Oberholtzer: It's about the book, and he's leaving town. I won't be long. I'll just grab my coat.

Mrs. Oberholtzer: Take a hat, dear.

Madge Oberholtzer: No time, Mother. I'll see you later.

Narrator 2: The next morning, the phone rings in the home of Asa J. Smith, an attorney and friend of the Oberholtzers. Smith listens to Mrs. Oberholtzer describe how Madge left the night before—and never returned.

Asa J. Smith: She's probably just fine, Mrs. Oberholtzer. But let me investigate this a bit. I'll call you right back.

Narrator 1: Smith heads downtown to confer with a friend. Familiar with rumors about Stephenson's many women friends, he still can't imagine that Madge might have been abducted. Later, he checks in with Madge's mother.

Mrs. Oberholtzer: I'm so glad you called! We just got a telegram that they were driving through to Chicago and she'll be back on the night train.

Narrator 2: That night Smith and his friend wait at Union Station. Neither Madge nor Stephenson arrives. They go with Mrs. Oberholtzer to Stephenson's house where they are told that Mr. Stephenson's whereabouts are unknown.

THE TRIAL OF DAVID C. STEPHENSON

Narrator 1: By Tuesday morning, Mr. and Mrs. Oberholtzer tell their story to Detective Harry C. Webster. When they return home, they find Madge is back—though she is barely alive. Smith talks to Eunice Schultz, a boarder at the house.

Asa J. Smith: What happened, Eunice?

Eunice Schultz: I was the only one at home. I was in the kitchen. I heard groaning and I went to the dining room and saw Madge being carried upstairs by a large man. I stayed downstairs till the man came down.

Asa J. Smith: Did he say anything?

Eunice Schultz: He said she was hurt in an automobile accident. He said he thought no bones were broken.

Asa J. Smith: Who was he?

Eunice Schultz: He said his name was Johnson. Then he hurried down the stairs. He tried to hide his face and said he must hurry. I saw a big car parked by the driveway. Then I went to see Madge.

Asa J. Smith: How was she?

Eunice Schultz: She was groaning with every breath. I saw her bruises. On the right cheek was a circular wound. It was dark in color. There was a bruise on her left chest of the same shape, only deeper. It was an open wound. She just groaned and said, "Dear Mother."

Asa J. Smith: Did she say anything else?

Eunice Schultz: Yes, she said she thought she was dying and asked me to call Dr. Kingsbury. He's with her now.

Scene 4

Narrator 2: Dr. John K. Kingsbury finds Madge in a state of shock. She is cold, has a bruise on her cheek, and lacerations on her chest. The doctor knows her condition is grave and gently prods her to tell what happened.

Madge Oberholtzer: I was taken to Mr. Stephenson's house late Sunday night. I could tell he had been drinking and I asked to be taken home. He said I would be staying.

Dr. Kingsbury: Did you try to leave?

Madge Oberholtzer: I went to the telephone to call home. But one of the men took the phone from me. I tried again later, but they wouldn't let me call. Some men were drinking in the kitchen. They forced me to take two or three drinks. I got nauseous and stayed in a chair. They said I'd be going to Chicago with them and I started to cry.

Dr. Kingsbury: Did you go with them?

Madge Oberholtzer: Yes. They forced me into to go with them to Union Station. We boarded a train. I was still feeling ill from the drinks. I don't remember all of what happened, but I remember this. Stephenson forced me into a private compartment and attacked me. He held me so I could not move.

Dr. Kingsbury: What happened when you got to Chicago?

Madge Oberholtzer: We got off the train in Hammond and went to a hotel. I was desperate and almost used his gun to end it all. Then I came up with another plan. I begged Stephenson to let me buy a hat and some cosmetics. One of his men took me out and I got a black hat.

Dr. Kingsbury: Did you get the cosmetics, Madge?

Madge Oberholtzer: No. Instead I bought a box of mercury bichloride tablets and slipped them into my pocket.

Dr. Kingsbury: Madge, did you take some of the poison? Is that why you're so ill?

Madge Oberholtzer: I meant to take all of them. I thought that if I got sick enough they'd take me home or get me some help. I took six of them and couldn't get any more down. My stomach was too upset. I started vomiting. I think I may have fainted.

Dr. Kingsbury: What did Stephenson do when he found out?

Madge Oberholtzer: He had me drink some milk. He put me in the car and started driving. He refused to take me to a hospital. I even begged them to leave me at the side of the road where someone might find me and take me for help. Finally, we got to his home and he took me to some rooms above his garage.

Dr. Kingsbury: How did Stephenson act?

Madge Oberholtzer: He was upset, pacing and yelling. At one point he said I would have to marry him. That he was the law and the power. This morning Stephenson calmed down some, and the man named Earl said he was going to bring me home.

Narrator 1: Dr. Kingsbury begins to work on Madge, flushing out her stomach and covering her with blankets to warm her body temperature. Madge hovers between life and death.

Scene 5

Narrator 2: While Madge fights for her life, Asa J. Smith consults with her parents about charging Stephenson with assault and kidnapping. She repeats her story of the attack to Smith, and her parents give Smith the go-ahead to pursue a lawsuit against Stephenson. Smith and an associate visit Stephenson in his office.

Asa J. Smith: The matter we wish to talk to you about, Mr. Stephenson, is concerning Miss Madge Oberholtzer. We have been employed to bring suit against you for responsibility for her condition.

D. C. Stephenson: To bring suit. Well, I'll tell you, I've stood an awful lot of persecution. I am not looking for trouble, and would prefer to avoid it. But I am a scrapper. I've stood already more than any other human being, I suspect, but I can stand more.

Asa J. Smith: You may have stood more than any other human being, save one.

D. C. Stephenson: And who might that be?

Asa J. Smith: Miss Madge Oberholtzer.

D. C. Stephenson: Is this conversation personal or professional?

Asa J. Smith: Professional.

D. C. Stephenson: Then my attorneys will see you in your office this afternoon.

Narrator 1: During the next several days the attorneys for the Oberholtzers and Stephenson meet over a possible out-of-court settlement. Then, nine days after Madge returned home, Dr. Kingsbury tells the family that Madge is dying.

Narrator 2: Smith recommends that Madge's statement be committed to paper and prepared for her signature. Pages of notes are typed, reviewed, and corrected. Then a notary verifies Madge's signature on the detailed deathbed statement.

Narrator 1: Madge lingers until the morning of April 14. Four days later D. C. Stephenson is behind bars, along with Earl Gentry and Earl Klinck, who were with Stephenson during Madge's abduction.

Scene 6

Narrator 2: On October 12, 1925, Judge Will Sparks presides over jury selection in the Hamilton County Courtroom. Sixteen days later a total of 260 men have been interviewed. The jury is finally selected and the trial of Stephenson, Gentry, and Klinck begins. Charles Cox, attorney and former judge, opens for the prosecution.

Charles Cox: This is not an ordinary murder case. Usually murder is a deed of hate, of revenge, a deed committed with a gun, a knife, or a bludgeon. This was murder committed by a man, aided by his two satellites, a man who, the evidence will show, said, "I am the law in Indiana." This case is to determine whether we are to protect the sanctity of the honor and chastity of womanhood.

The State's main witness will be none other than Madge Oberholtzer, clean of soul, but with her bruised, mangled, poisoned body standing by her grave's edge. She will tell you the story of her entrapment, of her being drugged, kidnapped, assaulted, beaten, and finally driven to take the deadly poison that contributed to her untimely death.

Narrator 1: Will Remy, an attorney for the prosecution, questions Mrs. Oberholtzer about Madge's departure and return home. Dr. John Kingsbury describes her condition.

Will Remy: Did Madge say anything at first?

Dr. Kingsbury: She said she wanted to die. I had to press her to tell me what happened.

Narrator 2: Dr. Kingsbury then repeats Madge's story to the courtroom.

Will Remy: From the appearance of the lacerations, would you say they might have been bites by human teeth?

Dr. Kingsbury: In my opinion they were.

Narrator 1: A key strategy for the prosecution is to demonstrate that Madge might have recovered if she had received immediate medical attention, and if a bite had not become infected. The defense objects to this line of questioning, but to its dismay, the judge allows this to be explored.

Will Remy: In your opinion, what would have been the prospects for recovery if she had had medical aid four or five hours after she took the poison?

Dr. Kingsbury: Her chances would have been better.

Narrator 2: Remy questions Asa Smith about the preparation of Madge's statement, which prompts intense cross-examination by defense attorney Ephraim Inman. During the next few days the prosecution calls a variety of witnesses who testify that Madge was seen in the company of the defendants on the train and at the Indiana Hotel.

Narrator 1: Next, the prosecution calls Dr. Virgil H. Moon, an instructor of pathology at the Indiana University School of Medicine. Dr. Moon assisted with the autopsy.

Charles Cox: What are the chances for recovery from bicholoride of mercury poisoning?

Dr. Moon: Many cases have recovered. It isn't uniformly fatal.

Charles Cox: Describe the abscess found in the lungs.

Dr. Moon: This abscess consisted of pus. It also showed the presence of germs we call staphylococci.

Charles Cox: Did your examination disclose any injury that might have caused this infection?

Dr. Moon: I found only one area from which such an infection could have originated.

Charles Cox: Tell what it was.

Dr. Moon: The laceration on her chest was the only injury that could have caused the infection.

Charles Cox: Could such an injury be caused by human teeth?

Dr. Moon: It could be. Yes.

Charles Cox: Did this laceration show evidence of infection?

Dr. Moon: It showed evidence unmistakably.

Charles Cox: Are wounds made by biting usually infected?

Dr. Moon: They are very apt to be infected.

Charles Cox: What in your opinion was the cause of death?

Dr. Moon: Death resulted from a complication rather than from the direct effect of the mercuric chloride poisoning. The nature of the complication is the staph infection.

Narrator 2: After calling a few more witnesses to testify to the effects of the poisoning and infection, the State rests its case. The prosecution has played its most important card. If Dr. Moon is correct, Madge's death was not suicide. Stephenson killed her with his own teeth.

Scene 7

Narrator 1: The defense begins by calling doctors to testify about the effects of the poison, emphasizing the position that Madge caused her own death. Charles Cox vigorously leads the cross-examination. Then defense attorney Ira Holmes calls a mystery witness, Cora Householder.

Ira Holmes: Did you know Madge Oberholtzer?

Cora Householder: Yes, I've known her for several years.

Ira Holmes: Can you tell us where you live in proximity to the Oberholtzer home?

Cora Householder: I live at 5850 Beechwood Avenue, a few blocks from the Oberholtzer home.

Ira Holmes: Do you live with your husband?

Cora Householder: We are separated.

Ira Holmes: Where does your husband work?

Cora Householder: At the police station.

Ira Holmes: Did you ever see Madge Oberholtzer at the police station?

Narrator 2: Remy stands to object and the judge agrees that the question is not pertinent. Holmes takes a different angle.

Ira Holmes: Tell the jury whether your husband, at any time, lived at the Oberholtzer home.

Cora Householder: He did.

Ira Holmes: How long did he live in the Oberholtzer home?

Narrator 1: Again the defense objects.

Ira Holmes: State to the jury whether at any time you saw Madge Oberholtzer with your husband.

Narrator 2: The judge upholds the prosecution's objection and agrees to listen to Holmes's justification for his line of questioning outside the hearing of the jury. The many reporters in the courtroom, however, listen to Holmes's efforts to show that Madge may have had a relationship with Mrs. Householder's husband. Judge Sparks refuses to allow any testimony about Madge's character—there will be no mudslinging in his court. And the jury would continue to view Madge as an unsullied victim.

Narrator 1: In another attempt to demonstrate that Madge was more worldly than portrayed by the prosecution, the defense calls another witness, Dr. Vallery Ailstock, a dentist from Columbus, Indiana. Dr. Ailstock, a Klan organizer, has known Stephenson for three years.

Ira Holmes: Did you ever meet Madge Oberholtzer?

Dr. Ailstock: I met her in January of 1925 in Columbus.

Ira Holmes: Please describe the meeting.

Dr. Ailstock: I was standing on the corner of Fifth and Washington Streets, talking with Dr. Clawson, a friend of mine. A large automobile drove by and stopped. It was Mr. Stephenson. We stepped over to the curbing and shook hands with him. Then he introduced us to Miss Oberhotlzer.

Ira Holmes: What else did you discuss?

Dr. Ailstock: I invited Mr. Stephenson to go fishing. Then Miss Oberholtzer asked us about getting liquor. I told her that I don't have an alcohol permit. She said something about how I should have alcohol, that it would make good gin.

Ira Holmes: Did you see her after that?

Dr. Ailstock: I saw her once after that in Stephenson's office. She was sitting in the reception room.

Narrator 2: The defense brings other witnesses in an effort to demonstrate that Madge had a longstanding relationship with Stephenson. They close with efforts to show that the staph infection could have been introduced by other means, such as the blood transfusion she received before she died. The defense rests its case.

Scene 8

Narrator 1: Closing arguments begin with Will Remy.

Will Remy: Gentlemen of the jury . . . Madge Oberholtzer is dead. She would be alive today if it were not for the unlawful acts of David C. Stephenson, Earl Klinck, and Earl Gentry. They destroyed her body. They tried to destroy her soul. And here in the past few days they have attempted to befoul her character. But they were unable to break down her story. Her statement stands forth as the truth.

Narrator 2: Stephenson, Klinck, and Gentry sit quietly while Remy goes on speaking for three hours. Then Remy concludes.

Will Remy: This girl's life might have been saved. But there was an abscess on her lung, brought on by the fangs of D. C. Stephenson.

Narrator 1: Ira Holmes begins his summation by emphasizing the lack of direct evidence, deeming Madge's death a suicide.

Ira Holmes: Suicide is not a crime in Indiana. Therefore, to be an accessory before or after the fact would be no crime in Indiana. There is the dying declaration. But why didn't she make an outcry when she was taken through Union Station? She was allowed to purchase a hat and went into a drug store, unguarded, and bought the poison. Couldn't she have gotten help at that time? This proves she wasn't abducted. Further, we have done nothing to blacken her character any more than presenting the evidence of what she did during her life serves to blacken her character. If you find Stephenson guilty of murder, you must find that he forced her to take poison. There is no evidence like that.

Narrator 2: Charles Cox gives the state's second closing argument.

Charles Cox: The law says that if murder is committed in the act of committing a rape or by the administering of or causing poison to be administered, that one of the penalties shall be death. If these men can take away a lady, entrap her, defile her, bite her, and kill her, these men should be killed by the law. They did not intend to kill her, perhaps. But they are liable criminally. They killed her, murdered her, and now they would write the scarlet letter on her tomb. These degenerates would go free to commit other outrages. But you won't let them do it. I think I know what is in the hearts of good men.

Narrator 1: Floyd Christian provides more of the defense's closing argument.

Floyd Christian: If a man went home and committed suicide because his banker refused to lend him money, you wouldn't hang the banker. It would be a plain case of suicide, as this is. Suicide can't be homicide and homicide can't be suicide. They are as different as black is from white.

Narrator 2: Ephraim Inman continues the arguments for the defense.

Ephraim Inman: Why didn't Madge tell the druggist of her plight? Where is the milliner from whom she bought the hat? There is not a lawyer in Indiana who wouldn't say that this prosecution for murder is entirely without justification. Not only that, but every cool-headed, fair-minded man you might meet upon the street feels that the defendants might be guilty of something, but they are not guilty of murder or homicide. The sole question is: Can suicide be murder? Can suicide be homicide? The law doesn't say it can be and never will say so.

Narrator 1: After more impassioned arguments from the prosecution, the judge provides his instructions to the jury. Following lunch the jurors begin their deliberations. At 5:21 P.M., the jurors return to the courtroom to announce their verdict.

Narrator 2: And now, you the audience must weigh the facts as you have heard them. As in all murder trials, you must agree upon your verdict. Are D. C. Stephenson, Earl Klinck, and Earl Gentry guilty of murder? You may deliberate the fate of each man individually.

Scene 9

Narrator 1: D. C. Stephenson is found guilty of murder in the second degree. Klinck and Gentry are found innocent. Stephenson fully expects that his friend Ed Jackson, who is governor of Indiana, will pardon him. However, the governor recognizes the political dangers of such a move and does not grant a pardon.

Narrator 2: During the next thirty-one years, Stephenson repeatedly files petitions for a new trial. In 1950, Governor Henry Schricker grants parole. However, Stephenson violates his parole agreement when he takes a job in Robbinsdale, Minnesota, and fails to report to his parole officer in Illinois. He is returned to prison until Governor George N. Craig grants a complete discharge on December 20, 1956.

Narrator 1: Stephenson marries his third wife, Martha Dickinson, but they separate in 1961. He moves to Jonesboro, Tennessee, in 1963 and marries Martha Murray Sutton while still legally married to Martha Dickinson. He dies on June 28, 1966, at the age of seventy-four.

8
In Defense of Home

The People of Michigan vs. Ossian Sweet et al.

Ossian Sweet, defendant for murder. Courtesy of the Burton Historical Collection, Detroit Public Library.

INTRODUCTION

During 1910 there were approximately 6,000 African Americans living in Detroit, a city of approximately 250,000. By 1925, the African American population had grown to approximately 80,000. Some neighborhoods were segregated, and organizations sprang up among white people to protect their neighborhoods from integration. During this volatile time, Dr. Ossian Sweet, a well-educated African American, and his wife and daughter bought a house on the corner of Charlevoix and Garland Avenues. Although this was a working class neighborhood made up of renters—hardly people whose property values would be harmed—residents resorted to intimidation to oust the Sweets. After an evening of rocks being thrown against the house, one or more shots rang out. Henry Sweet, Ossian's brother, returned fire. One man was wounded and another was killed. (Reports of what actually happened varied, but this seems to be the most corroborated version.) All eleven people who were in the Sweet home were arrested and prosecuted for murder. In the trial, there was more testimony available for the defense than for the prosecution. Most of the prosecution's witnesses (seventy-one) centered on whether there was truly an unruly crowd. This testimony has been collapsed into a few witnesses. Note that the use of terms such as *colored* and *Negroes* has been left in the testimony to be consistent with the times.

PRESENTATION SUGGESTIONS

The Sweet family, their friends, and the defense attorneys can sit on a row of chairs. The neighbors, angry man, police inspector, and prosecuting attorneys can stand behind them. The narrators and judge can stand to one side. Witnesses and neighbors can dress in street clothes. The attorneys and the Sweets can be in suits.

RELATED BOOK

Weinberg, Kenneth G. *A Man's Home, A Man's Castle*. New York: McCall Publishing Company, 1971.

THE PEOPLE OF MICHIGAN VS. OSSIAN SWEET ET AL.

CHARACTERS

Narrator 1

Narrator 2

Ossian Sweet, *an African-American doctor*

Gladys Sweet, *Ossian's wife*

Henry Sweet, *Ossian's brother*

Otis Sweet, *Ossian's brother*

Joe Mack, *Ossian's friend*

Angry Man

Norton Schuknecht, *police inspector*

Lestor S. Moll, *assistant prosecuting attorney*

Arthur Garfield Hays, *defense attorney*

Florence Ware, *a white neighbor*

Clarence Darrow, *renowned defense attorney*

Witness 1, *a white neighbor (a boy of sixteen)*

Witness 2, *a white neighbor*

Eben Draper, *a white neighbor*

Alfred Andrews, *a white neighbor*

Robert Toms, *prosecuting attorney*

Judge Frank Murphy

In Defense of Home

The People of Michigan vs. Ossian Sweet et al.

Scene 1

Narrator 1: In 1925, Detroit has seen a tremendous increase in its black population. Most of the nearly 80,000 blacks live on the east side, in an overcrowded area called Paradise Valley or Black Bottom.

Narrator 2: Dr. Ossian Sweet, a well-educated physician, his wife Gladys, and their daughter, Iva, have moved to Detroit. Gladys, a teacher, married Ossian in 1922, and they spent a year in Paris were he worked under Madame Curie.

Narrator 1: Now, Dr. Sweet has accepted a position on the staff at Detroit's first black hospital. After spending the winter with Gladys's parents, the young couple has been searching for a house of their own.

Ossian Sweet: Gladys, I may have found us a good house.

Gladys Sweet: Tell me about it, Ossian.

Ossian Sweet: It's a bungalow, but it seems to be of good construction, with some brick. There's a sizable front porch and lots of windows.

Gladys Sweet: What is the neighborhood like?

Ossian Sweet: There's a grocery store across the street. There's a school on the other corner, so it will be convenient for Iva someday. It's on the corner, and it's probably the nicest house in the area. There's also an apartment house nearby.

Gladys Sweet: An apartment house? I'm not sure about that.

Ossian Sweet: Well, you need to see the house before you make up your mind.

Gladys Sweet: What about the people there?

Ossian Sweet: It's a white neighborhood. Does that bother you?

Gladys Sweet: Not really. My family was surrounded by whites on our block for years. Our friends won't be our neighbors anyway, probably. Let's take a look at it.

Narrator 2: As Ossian expected, Gladys finds the house to be attractive and exactly right for their young family.

Gladys Sweet: Ossian, this is just what we need! Can we afford it?

Ossian Sweet: Yes, Gladys. I'll start the loan application.

Gladys Sweet: And I'll start planning how to decorate it!

Scene 2

Narrator 1: The Sweets buy their house, completing the purchase in June. Dr. Sweet delays moving in that summer. He discusses his reasons for the delay with his brothers, Otis, a dentist, and Henry, a college student.

Henry Sweet: When are you moving into your new house, brother?

Ossian Sweet: I'm worried about moving in.

Otis Sweet: Why? I thought everything was all set.

Ossian Sweet: Oh, the loan went through okay. That's fine. Gladys is planning where to put everything. But there have been rumors of trouble in that neighborhood.

Henry Sweet: What do you mean?

Ossian Sweet: The neighbors don't want to be integrated.

Otis Sweet: What could they possibly have to complain about?

Ossian Sweet: They claim the property values will drop.

Henry Sweet: But aren't most of them renters? That's an apartment house across the street.

Ossian Sweet: That doesn't seem to matter. These people hate to see things change.

Henry Sweet: I heard about the home bought by Dr. Alexander Turner. His trouble started when the moving van arrived.

Otis Sweet: What happened?

Henry Sweet: A crowd gathered and they broke out the windows with bricks and rocks. Then some men came from the Tireman Avenue Improvement Association asking Turner to sell the house back to them. He sold. . . .

Ossian Sweet: I've heard that they've started a similar organization in our neighborhood—the Waterworks Improvement Association.

Otis Sweet: And what about the Fletcher family? Didn't they have a lot of trouble?

Ossian Sweet: Yes, it was the same sort of rock and brick throwing. But someone got shot and the Fletchers were arrested. They weren't in that house long.

Otis Sweet: Well, Ossian, what are you going to do?

Ossian Sweet: I think I'm going to wait for the summer to end. Maybe when the weather's better people won't be as likely to make trouble.

Henry Sweet: You sure you don't want to walk away from this?

Ossian Sweet: You know what we grew up with in Florida. I can still see that mob pouring kerosene on Fred Rochelle and setting fire to him. And the lynchings. . . . Surely we've come away from that.

Otis Sweet: Well, let us know when you're ready. We're behind you—if you are sure you want to do this.

Ossian Sweet: Look, you know I can't walk away from it. I have to die as a man or live as a coward.

Scene 3

Narrator 2: On September 8th, two small vans bring the Sweet's possessions to their new home on Garland and Charlevoix Avenues. Ossian also brings guns and ammunition. Otis and Henry join him, along with several family friends. The first night is fairly peaceful. Six policemen have been notified about the Sweets' planned move-in, and they keep people from lingering in front of the house.

Narrator 1: Gladys has hired a man to help with the move. While Ossian goes to his office on September 9th, Gladys supervises some of their friends with the settling in and makes plans for furniture purchases.

Narrator 2: Late that afternoon, one of the men notices that people are repeatedly passing by, pausing to look at the house. The crowd gathers so rapidly that two of Gladys's friends decide to spend the night with the Sweets. They are afraid to depart through the crowd. When Ossian arrives home, he is hit by a rock as he pushes his way through the crowd to his front door.

Narrator 1: Gladys prepares dinner while Ossian and his friends play cards. Joe Mack expresses his concern over the hostility.

Joe Mack: That crowd is getting larger and more restless, Ossian.

Ossian Sweet: It's a hot evening. Maybe they'll go inside once it cools off a bit.

Joe Mack: Are the police coming back?

Ossian Sweet: Yes, there are several officers outside.

Joe Mack: I don't know how much good they are going to be if things get out of hand.

Narrator 2: Gladys continues to fix dinner, reminding the men that she'll need the card table they are using when it's time to eat. Shortly before eight o'clock, Otis and a friend, William Davis, arrive by taxi.

Angry Man: Look! There's more of them! Get them! Get them!

Narrator 1: The two men hurry inside.

Otis Sweet: There are hundreds of people out there, Ossian! Pull down the blinds!

Narrator 2: The Sweets pull the shades and turn out the lights. There are now eleven people in the Sweet house. They wait nervously, hoping the police, who have been nearby throughout the evening, will disperse the crowd.

Ossian Sweet: Gladys, I don't think we are going to be able to eat dinner tonight. Men, let's get the guns and be ready in case there's trouble. There are several policemen outside, but I don't think five or six policemen can hold out against that mob if they storm the house.

Otis Sweet: Ladies, stay away from the windows. Let's see if we can get through the night.

Narrator 1: Sometime after eight o'clock, a hail of rocks hits the house. One rock smashes out an upstairs window. Then the Sweets hear a gunshot or two and someone from the house returns fire. A short time later, Inspector Norton Schuknecht enters the house.

Norton Schuknecht: What are you fellows shooting at?

Ossian Sweet: We're just protecting our home.

Norton Schuknecht: Well, stop! You can't shoot into that crowd like that.

Ossian Sweet: Yes, sir. We'll put up our arms.

Narrator 2: A short time later, Schuknecht returns.

Norton Schuknecht: I need all of you to come to police headquarters with me.

Ossian Sweet: Why? What has happened?

Norton Schuknecht: No discussion now. Just come with me.

Narrator 1: The family and friends of the Sweets discover at police headquarters that Eric Houghberg received a bullet wound to his leg and that Leon Breiner, age thirty-three, has been killed by gunfire. The assistant prosecutor recommends that all eleven people be charged with first-degree murder.

Scene 4

Narrator 2: Although exhausted from the Scopes Monkey trial, the famous defense attorney Clarence Darrow agrees to lead the defense for the trial that opens on October 30, 1925. Darrow is impressed with the presiding judge, Frank Murphy, and believes that he will be fair.

Narrator 1: For five weeks, Darrow questions 150 potential jurors, trying to find twelve men who say they can be fair. All the jurors are white.

Narrator 2: Lester Moll, assistant prosecuting attorney, opens the case.

Lestor S. Moll: Ladies and gentleman of the jury, this is a case about a peaceful neighborhood where lives were shattered when the defendants loosed an unprovoked barrage of gunfire on innocent people. Some will say it's a case about blacks having a right to live where they choose. I agree that they have a civil right to live wherever they choose. However, a more important right is that of a person to live. Leon Breiner lost that right on September 9th. He lost that right when he stood on a neighbor's porch, amiably smoking his pipe. This is not a case about racial prejudice. It's a case of premeditated murder.

Narrator 1: Clarence Darrow ostentatiously works on a crossword puzzle during Moll's opening remarks. Then Arthur Garfield Hays opens for the defense.

Arthur Garfield Hays: The right of self-defense in our history is centuries old. Self-defense is a necessary feature of organized society. It is the dearest right of a free man. But the right of self-defense cannot be an excuse for wantonly taking human life. You, gentlemen of the jury, will learn the facts as they appeared from inside that little house—the facts as they appeared to eleven people of the black race who were affected by knowledge of the appalling treatment of their race. The question is what a colored man, with his knowledge that people had threatened to bomb his home and kill him if he moved into the neighborhood, would do. Our theory is self-defense and we claim the law to be that one is justified in defending himself when he believes that his life is in danger.

Narrator 2: The prosecution calls a variety of witnesses to testify that the few people outside the Sweet home were quiet and not a threat to the Sweets.

Lestor S. Moll: Mrs. Ware, how close do you live to the Sweets?

Florence Ware: I live two blocks away.

Lestor S. Moll: Did you notice anything unusual?

Florence Ware: People seemed to be enjoying the summer evening.

Narrator 1: Clarence Darrow cross-examines Mrs. Ware.

Clarence Darrow: Why did you go to the corner of Garland and Charlevoix?

Florence Ware: I was curious.

Clarence Darrow: Curious about what?

Florence Ware: The crowd . . . I mean there wasn't really a crowd. I was just curious.

Narrator 2: Another witness, a boy of sixteen, struggles when cross-examined by Darrow.

Clarence Darrow: What did you see at the corner of Garland and Charlevoix?

Witness 1: There was a great crowd—no, I won't say a great crowd, a large crowd—well there were a few people there and the officers were keeping them moving.

Clarence Darrow: Have you talked to anyone about this case?

Witness 1: Lieutenant Johnson.

Clarence Darrow: And when you started to answer the question you forgot to say "a few people" didn't you?

Witness 1: Yes sir.

Narrator 1: Dozens of witnesses for the prosecution insist there were not any crowds the night of the shooting.

Lestor S. Moll: What brought you to that corner?

Witness 2: Curiosity.

Lestor S. Moll: About what?

Witness 2: Nothing in particular.

Lestor S. Moll: Were there many people there?

Witness 2: Some.

Lestor S. Moll: How many?

Witness 2: Twenty-five or thirty.

Scene 5

Narrator 2: In addition to countering the prosecution's claims that there were few people outside the Sweet house, Clarence Darrow probes witnesses about their membership in the Waterworks Improvement Association. He questions Eben Draper.

Clarence Darrow: Did the Sweet's purchase of the house have anything to do with your joining the club?

Eben Draper: Yes.

Clarence Darrow: You joined the club to aid keeping that a white district.

Eben Draper: Yes.

Clarence Darrow: At the meeting in the school, was any reference made to keep the district free from colored people?

Eben Draper. Yes.

Clarence Darrow: How many people were present at that meeting?

Eben Draper: Seven hundred.

Narrator 1: Alfred Andrews describes the pep talk a man from the Tireman Improvement Association gave to the Waterworks Improvement Association.

Clarence Darrow: Did the speaker tell you about any race riot trouble they had in his neighborhood?

Alfred Andrews: Yes, he told us about a Negro named Dr. Turner who had bought a house on Spokane Avenue.

Clarence Darrow: Did he say his organization made Turner leave?

Alfred Andrews: Yes. He said his organization wouldn't have Negroes in their neighborhood and that they would cooperate with us in keeping them out of ours.

Clarence Darrow: Did the crowd applaud him?

Alfred Andrews: Yes.

Clarence Darrow: Did you applaud?

Alfred Andrews: Yes.

Clarence Darrow: You feel that way now?

Alfred Andrews: Yes, I haven't changed.

Clarence Darrow: You know a colored man has certain rights?

Alfred Andrews: Yes, I was in favor of keeping the Sweets out by legal means.

Clarence Darrow: Did the speaker talk of legal means?

Alfred Andrews: No, he was a radical. I myself do not believe in violence.

Clarence Darrow: Did anyone in that audience of five hundred or more people protest against the speaker's advocacy of violence?

Alfred Andrews: I don't know.

Scene 6

Narrator 2: Next, Inspector Norman Schuknecht testifies for the prosecution.

Lestor S. Moll: Were there people on the street when you arrived at about 7:30?

Norman Schuknecht: There were people on the street, but they were walking up and down and there was no congregating.

Lestor S. Moll: What instructions had you given your officers?

Norman Schuknecht: I told them Dr. Sweet could live there—even if we had to take every man in the police station to see that he did.

Lestor S. Moll: Did you see anyone armed with clubs or other weapons?

Norman Schuknecht: Not at any time.

Lestor S. Moll: What happened at 8:15?

Norman Schuknecht: Suddenly a volley of shots was fired from the windows of Dr. Sweet's home.

Lestor S. Moll: What could you see?

Norman Schuknecht: I saw flashes of guns.

Lestor S. Moll: How many shots?

Norman Schuknecht: About fifteen or twenty.

Narrator 1: Defense attorney Arthur Garfield Hays questions Ossian Sweet.

Arthur Garfield Hays: When did you first observe anything outside?

Ossian Sweet: We were playing cards. It was about eight o'clock when something hit the roof of the house.

Arthur Garfield Hays: What happened after that?

Ossian Sweet: Somebody went to the window and then I heard the remark, "The people, the people."

Arthur Garfield Hays: And then?

Ossian Sweet: I ran out to the kitchen where my wife was. There were several lights burning. I turned them out and opened the door. I heard someone yell, "Go and raise hell in front. I'm going back." I was frightened and, after getting a gun, ran upstairs. Stones kept hitting our house intermittently. I threw myself on the bed and lay there a short while. Perhaps fifteen minutes had passed, when a stone came through the window. Part of the glass hit me.

Arthur Garfield Hays: What happened then?

Ossian Sweet: Pandemonium—I guess that's the best way of describing it—broke loose. Everyone was running from room to room. There was a general uproar. Somebody yelled, "There's someone coming!" A car had pulled up to the curb. My brother and Mr. Davis got out. They yelled, "Here's the niggers! Get them! Get them!" As they rushed in, the mob surged forward fifteen or twenty feet. It looked like a human sea. Stones kept coming faster. I ran downstairs. Another window was smashed. Then I heard one shot. Then eight or ten came from upstairs. After that, it was all over.

Arthur Garfield Hays: Describe your state of mind at the time of the shooting.

Ossian Sweet: When I opened the door and saw the mob, I realized I was facing the same mob that had hounded my people throughout its entire history. In my mind, I was pretty confident of what I was up against, with my back against the wall. I was filled with a peculiar fear, the kind no one could feel unless they knew the history of our race. I knew what mobs had done to my people before.

Scene 7

Narrator 2: Clarence Darrow provides the summation for the defense.

Clarence Darrow: If I thought any of you had any opinion about the guilt of my clients, I wouldn't worry, because that might be changed. What I'm worried about is prejudice. I know that if these defendants had been a white group defending themselves from a colored mob, they never would have been arrested or tried. My clients are charged with murder, but what they are really charged with is being black. . . .

Every policeman knew that the crowd was after the Negroes. But no one batted an eye. Think how you would feel if you fired at some black man in a black community, and then had to be tried by them.

The danger of a mob is not what it does, but what it might do. The mob was waiting to see the sacrifice of some helpless blacks. They came with malice in their hearts.

The Sweets spent their first night in their home afraid to go to bed. The next night they spent in jail. Now the State wants them to spend the rest of their lives in the penitentiary. The State claims there was no mob there that night. Gentleman, the State has put on enough witnesses—more than seventy—who said they were there. Those witnesses alone would make a mob.

There are persons in the north and the south who say a black man is inferior to the white and should be controlled by the whites. There are also those who recognize his rights and say he should enjoy them. To me this case is a cross-section of human history. It involves the future and the hope of some of us that the future shall be better than the past.

Narrator 1: Robert Toms, prosecuting attorney, provides part of the summation for the prosecution.

Robert Toms: I have learned more about the race problem in this case than I ever knew. And I don't think there's a panacea for it. It isn't your business to settle it. Mr. Darrow would lead you to believe that the witnesses are lying about the people who gathered that evening. I never dreamed Mr. Darrow would have the nerve to come into this court and say every witness was a liar and a scoundrel.

What an insignificant figure Leon Breiner has been in this argument, and yet we started out to find out who killed him. Let's not forget that Breiner was killed because he was indiscreet enough to stop in front of a house where some Negroes wanted to live.

I concede the right of any man, black or white, to live where he likes or wherever he can afford to live. But we all have many civil rights that we voluntarily waive in the name of public peace, comfort, and security. There is one civil right more precious than all the others, which no man surrenders except at the command of God or his country, and that is the right to live. Let us ask ourselves, what has Leon Breiner done to have been deprived of that right?

Had he committed some outrage that his right to live should have been taken away from him, without his having the least chance to defend it? Did Breiner arm himself to protect his civil rights—his right to live? Which is more important—the right to live where you please or the right to live at all? Certainly Breiner, had he been given a chance to speak, would have said, "I'll live anywhere, but let me live...."

In spite of all arguments, the recounting of civil rights, the theory of race hatred—there lies the body of Leon Breiner with a bullet hole in his back, his lips silent forever. You can't ignore that Leon Breiner, peacefully chatting with his neighbor at his doorstep, enjoying his God-given and inalienable right to live, was shot through the back from ambush. And you can't make anything out of these facts but cold-blooded murder.

Narrator 2: Judge Frank Murphy provides instructions to the jury.

Judge Frank Murphy: Only those defendants whose acts indicate individual responsibility can be found guilty.

Narrator 1: Based on the evidence, this limits the guilty possibilities to Ossian Sweet and Henry Sweet. Ossian could be found guilty because he was controlling his family and friends. Henry Sweet could be found guilty because on the night of the shooting he admitted firing the gun.

Judge Frank Murphy: When you deliberate, you must consider the defendants' race and color. Consider also, that a man's home is his castle whether he is white or black. Ask yourselves whether the Sweets had reasonable cause to sense danger. If such a belief existed, the shooting would be justifiable and the defendants should be found not guilty.

Narrator 2: And now, you the audience must weigh the facts as you have heard them. As in all murder trials, you must agree upon your verdict. Are Ossian Sweet and Henry Sweet guilty of killing Leon Breiner?

Scene 8

Narrator 1: All day long, rumors fly through the courthouse. The instructions from Judge Murphy seem to favor the defendants. Yet the jury deliberates for forty-six hours. Loud arguments can be heard from the jury room.

Narrator 2: Finally, the jury reports to Judge Murphy that they cannot reach agreement. The trial ends in a hung jury.

Narrator 1: Of course, that is not the end of the story. Let's hear from some of the key people to learn what happened next.

Clarence Darrow: In April of 1926, a second trial began. This time each defendant was to be tried individually. The first trial was against Henry Sweet. The testimony was essentially the same. I delivered an eight-hour speech for the summation, emphasizing that this was a case of prejudice more than a murder case. I was especially worried about one juror who showed no emotion throughout the trial. I wondered if he was for or against us. The verdict came in only four hours later—not guilty. I later learned that this juror had walked into the jury room, lit a cigar, opened a book, and told the rest not to bother him until there were ready to acquit Henry Sweet.

Ossian Sweet: In July 1927 all charges against the other defendants were dropped.

Gladys Sweet: Our daughter died of tuberculosis two years after the trial.

Ossian Sweet: Leon Breiner's widow sued us for wrongful death in 1927. I don't think Gladys could stand the stress. She died two years later, also of tuberculosis. Henry died of the same disease in 1940.

Clarence Darrow: Ossian Sweet committed suicide on March 19, 1960.

9

Evading the Truth

The United States of America vs. Al Capone

Al Capone, *right,* defendant in a trial for income tax evasion, with attorney **Michael Ahern**. AP Photo.

INTRODUCTION

Prohibition, dictated by the passage of the Eighteenth Amendment to the U.S. Constitution, was in full swing during the 1920s. The law prohibited the sale of liquor, but provided exceptions for liquor sold for medicinal, sacramental, or industrial use. The rich, who had anticipated prohibition, had filled their wine cellars and liquor cabinets. Others who were determined to consume alcohol had to resort to buying moonshine from illegal sources, often delivered by bootleggers who transported the moonshine. (The term *bootleggers,* popular in the 1890s, derived from the practice of concealing liquor in the upper part of the leg or boot.) The Volstead Act provided for enforcement of the amendment, however, the enforcers of the Eighteenth Amendment, the Internal Revenue of the Treasury Department, could not stop the criminals who found the sale of illegal alcohol an opportunity for rich rewards. One of those men was Al "Scarface" Capone, leader of the Chicago Mafia. Known for his rages—later attributed to a form of dementia caused by syphilis—Capone ran the Chicago rackets with a firm hand. Yet he consistently escaped conviction until George E. Q. Johnson, U.S. Attorney, and one of his agents, the better-known Eliot Ness, pursued him on income tax evasion. Students may enjoy researching Eliot Ness's life or watching old episodes of the television series, *The Untouchables*.

PRESENTATION SUGGESTIONS

The narrators can sit on stools to the side. Have Capone and all the characters associated with Capone sit in the first row: Jack McGurn, Fred "Killer" Burke, Claude Maddox, Mae Capone, Leslie Shumway, Fred Ries, Milton Held, and Budd Gentry. Have all the other characters sit on stools or stand on the second row, with the attorneys for each side grouped on either side of the judge: Eliot Ness, Emma Ness, Chester Bragg, Dwight Green, Jacob Grossman, James Herbert Wilkerson, George E. Q. Johnson, Michael Ahern, Albert Fink, and Foreman. Characters wear clothing appropriate to the 1920s and early 1930s.

RELATED BOOKS

Bergreen, Lawrence. *Al Capone: The Man and the Era.* New York: Simon and Schuster, 1994.

Grant, Robert, and Joseph Katz. *The Great Trials of the Twenties: The Watershed Decade in America's Courtrooms.* Rockville Centre, NY: Sarpedon, 1998.

King, David C. *Al Capone and the Roaring Twenties.* Farmington Hills, MI: The Gale Group, 1998.

MacDonald, Alan. *Al and His Gang.* New York: Scholastic, 2000.

CHARACTERS

Narrator 1

Narrator 2

Eliot Ness, *agent with the Federal Prohibition Department*

Emma Ness, *Eliot Ness's mother*

Al Capone, *defendant, Mafia leader, and alleged racketeer*

Jack McGurn, *Al Capone's bodyguard and partner*

Fred "Killer" Burke, *gunman*

Claude Maddox, *Al Capone's associate*

Mae Capone, *Al Capone's wife*

James Herbert Wilkerson, *judge*

Dwight Green, *prosecuting attorney*

Chester Bragg, *insurance agent*

Michael Ahern, *defense attorney*

Jacob Grossman, *prosecuting attorney*

Leslie Shumway, *bookkeeper for Capone's organization*

Fred Ries, *gambling cashier*

Albert Fink, *defense attorney*

Milton Held, *bookie*

Budd Gentry, *bookie*

George E. Q. Johnson, *U.S. Attorney*

Foreman

Evading the Truth

The United States of America vs. Al Capone

Scene 1

Narrator 1: It's 1928 and the Mafia seems to have taken control of Chicago. Their power is partly based on illegal liquor sales. The Eighteenth Amendment to the U.S. Constitution, which prohibited the buying and selling of alcohol, went into effect in January 1920. Illegal liquor, known as moonshine, is available in secret. A person just has to know where to buy.

Narrator 2: People who brew moonshine are called *moonshiners* and people who sell or transport moonshine are called *bootleggers*. A battle between legal and illegal forces has erupted across the nation, especially in larger cities like Chicago. There are three people who figure prominently in this battle. Al Capone, born in 1899 to Italian immigrants, was the leader of a gang in Brooklyn by the time he was fourteen and was head of the Mafia in Chicago by the time he was thirty.

Narrator 1: George E. Q. Johnson, a U.S. attorney in his mid-fifties, grew up in the Midwest where he developed his strong sense of justice. The third key player in this drama is Eliot Ness, a young man of age twenty-six, who was born to Norwegian immigrants in Chicago. Ness, who still lives at home, is very close to his mother.

Eliot Ness: Mother! I got the job! I'll be working in the Prohibition Department.

Emma Ness: Congratulations, Eliot! Tell me what you'll be doing.

Eliot Ness: I'll be working with Dan Koken, and we'll be trying to break up the Capone organization. Capone has stills all over the area. We're going to try to infiltrate the system so we can find out the locations of the stills and stop the bootleggers when they make their deliveries.

Emma Ness: That sounds dangerous, Son. Are you sure you want to do this?

Eliot Ness: Of course I do! Someone has to stop the Mafia—and we especially need to stop Al Capone. I'm going to start small—I've always wanted to work undercover. I'm pretty much unknown, so I should be able to find out a lot in no time.

Emma Ness: You know, I'm beginning to believe that without prohibition we'd have a lot less corruption.

Eliot Ness: What do you mean?

Emma Ness: A lot of people want to have a glass of wine or mug of beer. That's the way it's been all my life. Now that alcohol is illegal, people are going to find a way to get it. Getting liquor has become a big business. The crooks seem to be getting richer all the time.

Eliot Ness: You're right about that, Ma. Even some police benefit from it. So many of them take bribes—and that is why the Prohibition Department is so important. We have to destroy the system before it destroys the country.

Emma Ness: Just as long as you're not destroyed in the process, Son.

Eliot Ness: Don't worry about me, Ma. They can't touch me.

Scene 2

Narrator 2: Ness and Koken begin their work by frequenting a Chicago Heights saloon called the Cozy Corners. Bootleggers from the surrounding area gather there to drink and socialize, while members of the mob drive the cars off to be filled with moonshine. When the men go home, their cars are loaded.

Narrator 1: Ness and Koken shake down some of the drivers, posing as corrupt Prohibition agents. Before long, though, it's going bad. Ness finds himself explaining to his mother how his cover has been blown.

Eliot Ness: Ma, you don't have to worry about me working undercover anymore.

Emma Ness: What happened, Eliot?

Eliot Ness: Dan and I were doing pretty well. Everyone knew we were Prohibition agents, but figured we were crooks. We were taking in so many bribes we could have gotten rich! We actually took in thousands of dollars.

Emma Ness: Eliot! What did you do with the money?

Eliot Ness: We turned it all in to the boss, of course.

Emma Ness: All that money. Well, I see how tempted people must get.

Eliot Ness: Yeah, there's plenty of money in alcohol. But it can be deadly too.

Emma Ness: What do you mean?

Eliot Ness: I think you've met one of the agents, Burt Napoli. Well, he posed as my chauffeur. We had a meeting with Joseph Martino. We were going to insist on getting in on his rackets.

Emma Ness: Martino—I've heard about him. Wasn't he the leader of the old Phil Piazza gang? You know, the Sicilian gang. I thought Capone drove out that gang.

Eliot Ness: Martino's about the only one left. I thought he and Capone were on the same side of the street now, but I was wrong—dead wrong.

Emma Ness: How's that, Eliot?

Eliot Ness: Well, at our meeting with Martino, I asked about the other still owners. He said he was representing them and would be handling our pay. We tried to find out who else was on the take. We thought we might learn who from the Prohibition office was in on it. But we didn't get anywhere.

Emma Ness: Did they agree to anything?

Eliot Ness: Yes, $500 a week. I figured I had the main source figured out, so I ordered search warrants. We raided eighteen stills. Destroyed them and took a lot of prisoners.

Emma Ness: That's great news, Son! You should be pretty proud of yourself.

Eliot Ness: No, Ma. They didn't waste any time getting back at us. Burt Napoli, the agent who was posing as my chauffeur, was murdered.

Emma Ness: Oh, dear. I'm so sorry. Do you know who did it?

Eliot Ness: We arrested a suspect, but he used his necktie to hang himself in his cell.

Emma Ness: How awful! What's going to happen now?

Eliot Ness: Well, I can't work undercover anymore. And I'm going to have to be careful for a while. In fact—and here's the hard part, Ma—the police are going to put a guard on the house. And I think it might be best if I start to look for an apartment. I don't want to put you and Dad at risk.

Emma Ness: Son, are you sure this is all worth it?

Eliot Ness: Worth it? It's tough to think about losing Burt. But Ma, it's not safe out there. Someone has to stop these people.

Scene 3

Narrator 2: George E. Q. Johnson, Ness's boss, also believes that someone has to stop the Mafia. He zeroes in on Al Capone's power in Chicago Heights after its police chief, Leroy Gilbert, is killed while sitting in his home reading the newspaper. Gilbert was scheduled to testify against two bootleggers the following morning.

Narrator 1: Johnson wastes no time in sending a message to Al Capone. One month later, on January 6, 1929, one hundred deputies lead the largest raid ever seen in Chicago Heights. They first take over the jail to ensure a secure place for the men they anticipate arresting. Then they strike at the heart of the slot machine operation, housed on the estate of Oliver J. Ellis. Al Capone is outraged and talks with his bodyguard and partner, "Machine Gun" Jack McGurn a few days later.

Al Capone: This is a disaster! They destroyed hundreds of slot machines.

Jack McGurn: I know, boss. I hear that kids woke up and chased nickels and dimes all over the place.

Al Capone: At least the kids got something out of it. The only other good news is that Martino is finally out of the picture.

Jack McGurn: That Eliot Ness arrested him, didn't he?

Al Capone: Yeah, Jack. But he didn't have Martino for long. I would have loved to see his face when he found out that Martino was gunned down minutes after making bail. Serves them both right. Ness doesn't get his man and Martino gets what's coming to him.

Jack McGurn: If Ness had stayed out of this, Martino could have died an old man.

Al Capone: That's the least of our worries.

Jack McGurn: What do you mean?

Al Capone: I hear they got into the safe and found the ledgers.

Jack McGurn: So what? You got nothing to worry about, boss.

Al Capone: You're probably right. Ellis isn't talking, but I still wish they hadn't gotten those records. My brother is pretty involved in that business.

Jack McGurn: Hey, boss. Ralph can look out for himself.

Al Capone: You're right, Jack. Still, I think it might be time for me to spend a bit of time in Miami Beach.

Narrator 2: Capone was right to worry about the records. They reveal that the slot machines bring in $275,000 a year. The Internal Revenue Service takes particular interest in the records, noting that Ralph Capone had signed a check in the amount of $2,130, dated June 27, 1928.

Narrator 1: The IRS has long suspected that Ralph Capone made far more money than he reports. This gives them a reason to fully investigate his finances. Before long, the IRS has enough evidence to indict him for income tax evasion.

Narrator 2: Income tax evasion might not seem like a major sin in those days, but the authorities reason that if they can successfully convict Ralph Capone, they can go after a much bigger fish—Al Capone.

Scene 4

Narrator 1: While Al Capone is in Florida, he ignores Ralph's tax problems. He has bigger worries—the biggest in the form of George "Bugs" Moran, a rival racketeer, who has repeatedly tried to assassinate Capone.

Narrator 2: Bugs Moran decides to go after McGurn and sends two gunmen, Pete and Frank Gusenberg, to kill him. They follow McGurn to a phone booth and fire at him with a machine gun and revolver.

Narrator 1: McGurn lives—which is good news for Capone and bad news for the

Gusenberg brothers and Bugs Moran. As soon as McGurn has recovered, he talks to Capone by phone.

Al Capone: Jack, I think you must have nine lives! I don't know how you survived that shooting.

Jack McGurn: I guess I just live right, boss. But now I think it's time we get rid of that vermin. The Gusenbergs, Bugs—we need to take care of that problem permanently.

Al Capone: You're right, Jack. But I can't have anything to do with this. You know that. Ness and Andrews would like nothing better than to take me in on murder charges.

Jack McGurn: You just sit tight here, boss. I'll take care of it.

Narrator 2: McGurn takes his time studying the gang's movements. Then he assembles several gunmen from out of town. Fred "Killer" Burke will lead the gang. McGurn discusses his plans with Burke and Claude Maddox, an associate of Al Capone's.

Jack McGurn: Here's how it's going to go down. The gang operates out of a garage. Let's get them there with a load of whiskey.

Fred "Killer" Burke: How about some Old Log Cabin whiskey. They'll think they're getting Canadian whiskey, which is pretty profitable.

Jack McGurn: Perfect. Burke, they don't know you, so you can set up the delivery.

Fred "Killer" Burke: How about Valentine's Day? We'll give them a very *special* delivery.

Jack McGurn: *(chuckling)* I like the way you think.

Fred "Killer" Burke: How are we going to get into the garage?

Claude Maddox: That's the best part. I've gotten police uniforms for everyone. I'll "find" a police car for you.

Fred "Killer" Burke: I get it. They'll think it's a routine bust and we'll be in. What about you, Jack? No one knows us around here, but you'll need a good alibi.

Jack McGurn: My girl and I are going to spend some time at the Stevens Hotel. We'll make sure the staff knows where we are. This is a perfect plan, boys.

Narrator 1: At 10:30 on February 14, 1929, Bugs Moran arrives at the garage. Burke and the other gunmen put on their police uniforms and drive up in the stolen police car. They enter the garage and find the Gusenberg brothers and various other racketeers, including Bugs Moran's brother-in-law.

Narrator 2: Burke and three other gunmen order the men to line up against the wall with their hands raised. Assuming the gunmen are truly police officers, the racketeers comply and give up their weapons. Then the gunmen open fire with two machine guns, a .45 and a sawed-off shotgun. Frank Gusenberg, with twenty-two bullet wounds, is the only survivor. He dies within minutes of arriving at a hospital, refusing to identify the attackers.

Narrator 1: Bugs Moran isn't present at the St. Valentine's Day massacre. But he gets the message. He's never again as powerful in Chicago. Fearing a bloodbath, racketeers flee Chicago by the hundreds, with most moving to Florida. Meanwhile, Al Capone and Jack McGurn have airtight alibis.

Scene 5

Narrator 2: The press believes that Al Capone is behind the massacre. The public feeds on the publicity, demanding that Capone be brought to justice; but Capone actually enjoys the publicity, and invites journalists into his Florida home. He plays the role of retired millionaire with a flair.

Narrator 1: Meanwhile, the federal authorities continue to investigate Capone. The incoming president, Herbert Hoover, puts pressure on the attorney general's office to put Capone in jail. George E. Q. Johnson issues a subpoena to Capone, demanding that he appear before a federal grand jury in Chicago in March regarding the Chicago Heights raid. In spite of frequent public appearances, Capone and his doctor claim that he is too sick with recurrent pneumonia to travel to Chicago.

Narrator 2: J. Edgar Hoover, director of the Federal Bureau of Investigation, orders an investigation. Capone has slipped in—and out—of the courts successfully before, and he decides it's time to work the system again. He returns to Chicago, where he testifies regarding his income. Afterward, he calls his wife, Mae, in Florida and she asks about the hearing.

Mae Capone: What happened in court, Al?

Al Capone: Nothing to worry about, Mae. I wasn't there much more than an hour.

Mae Capone: What did they ask about?

Al Capone: They just wanted to know how I've made my money and if I'd paid my income taxes.

Mae Capone: Isn't that what they are after Ralph for?

Al Capone: Yes, but I'm not worried, and you shouldn't be either.

Mae Capone: I know, but I can't help but worry. I read the papers, Al. The journalists assume you were behind the Valentine's Day shooting and the attempts on Bugs's life. And they all write about the fancy hotels, our homes, even the fact that you dress so well.

Al Capone: Not everyone is after us. Lots of people are grateful for what I do. They know about the soup kitchens I support and how I help the poor.

Mae Capone: But the government might look at that as another example of how you have money to burn, dear.

Al Capone: Mae, I don't even write checks! How are they going to prove anything? The income tax law is a lot of bunk anyway. The government can't collect legal taxes from illegal money.

Mae Capone: I hope you're right. What's going to happen? Are they going to let you go? Will you have to pay something?

Al Capone: I told them it was possible I might have missed a payment here or there. I'm coming up with enough money to make them happy and they've as much as said I have immunity. My attorneys said I don't need to worry—the attorneys say they cut me a deal.

Mae Capone: Well, that's a relief.

Al Capone: I'll be home before you know it.

Narrator 1: Assuming the immunity deal will hold, Capone returns to Florida. He realizes that other men are vying for control of the rackets, when he hears word that he'll be eliminated. Acting impulsively and out of fear for his life, he goes to Philadelphia, where he carefully engineers an arrest on a weapons charge. For the first time in his colorful criminal career Capone faces imprisonment, but he believes that this act will keep him safe.

Narrator 2: Capone enjoys a comfortable cell in Eastern Penitentiary in Holmesburg, Pennsylvania, complete with rugs and a telephone. He works as a library file clerk and reads when he isn't seeing visitors.

Scene 6

Narrator 1: On March 17, 1930, after ten months in prison, Al Capone leaves Eastern Penitentiary. Capone now splits his time between Miami and Chicago, flaunting his freedom. Several weeks later, Eliot Ness discusses the Capone brothers with his mother.

Emma Ness: Son, I read in the papers that Al Capone got out of prison in March. Are you still trying to stop him and Ralph?

Eliot Ness: Yes, we put wiretaps on Ralph's phone. He gave us just enough information that we were able to shut down some more of his bootlegging operations.

Emma Ness: I saw that Ralph Capone lost his case. Is he going to prison?

Eliot Ness: His attorneys are trying to keep him out, but I think he'll eventually serve time. Johnson also indicted Frank Nitti for income tax evasion. He's another one of Al's boys. Just getting Ralph convicted means it's more likely that we can get Al put away for a long time.

Emma Ness: People seem to want him put away for good. But income tax evasion doesn't seem like such a big crime compared to his bootlegging and the rumors that he's had people killed.

Eliot Ness: The problem is in trying to make a conviction stick. He's been charged with crimes and always manages to get let off. If he can get put in prison for income tax evasion . . . well . . . at least it gets him off the streets. Did you read what Frank Loesch started?

Emma Ness: No, what? Who is he?

Eliot Ness: He's the head of the Chicago Crime Commission. He put together a list of hoodlums he considers public enemies. Who do you think is first on the list?

Emma Ness: That's easy. Al Capone.

Eliot Ness: Right. And Ralph is not far behind.

Emma Ness: Al Capone . . . Public Enemy Number 1. That's quite a distinction.

Eliot Ness: Creating this list is smart. It reminds the public just how important it is to put these crooks away. It's so frustrating, Ma. Capone's back in Florida again, thumbing his nose at us. . . .

Narrator 2: Being identified as Public Enemy Number 1 keeps the public focused on Capone, which is exactly what Loesch wants. George E. Q. Johnson keeps looking for a reason, any reason, to get Capone behind bars. Johnson gets a break in September 1930, when Fred Ries, one of Capone's cashiers, begins to talk to the authorities. He implicates Ralph Capone, Frank "The Enforcer" Nitti, and another of Al's men, Jack "Greasy Thumb" Guzik.

Narrator 1: With the convictions of Nitti and Guzik in the fall of 1930, the case against Capone becomes stronger. Capone steps up his soup kitchen charity work and seems to be popular with many people. Meanwhile, Ness discusses his promotion and new responsibilities with his mother.

Eliot Ness: Ma, with my promotion, I have been told to concentrate on stopping Capone's income stream.

Emma Ness: How are you going to do that?

Eliot Ness: I've been able to put together a crack team of men to help. They're some of the top agents in the country. I'm calling them the Untouchables.

Emma Ness: Hundreds of men have already tried to stop Capone. What are you going to do that's different?

Eliot Ness: I'm taking the time to really study his liquor business. I've already learned that he reuses his beer barrels, so we'll start with the empty barrels leaving the speakeasies. We'll trace them right back to Capone's brewery.

Narrator 2: Ness's strategy is successful and the Untouchables begin seizing trucks and equipment. Both Ness and Johnson escape assassination attempts with their increased visibility.

Narrator 1: By November 1930, Ralph Capone's appeals have failed and he's imprisoned. Meanwhile, Johnson finalizes his indictment against Capone for income tax evasion. Capone's attorneys think they still have a deal—that Capone would plead guilty for a reduced sentence. However, Judge Wilkerson refuses a deal, and the indictments are announced on June 5, 1931. Capone turns himself in, posts a $50,000 bail, and leaves.

Scene 7

Narrator 2: The trial for income tax evasion begins on October 6, 1931. Everyone in the courtroom of Judge James Herbert Wilkerson notes Capone's impeccable dress, in spite of being overweight and beefy—and his confidence. Indeed, Capone calmly assumes his organization has ensured that the jury will see things his way. Judge Wilkerson's first order shakes Capone's confidence.

James Herbert Wilkerson: Good morning. Judge Edwards has another trial beginning today. Bailiff, take my entire panel of jurors to Judge Edwards. Bring me his jurors.

Narrator 1: Capone watches rigidly while Judge Wilkerson begins selecting the final jurors. Wilkerson then rules that the jury will be confined at night to ensure that there will be no possibility of bribes.

Narrator 2: On the morning of October 7th, prosecuting attorney Dwight Green calls their first witness, Chester Bragg, an insurance agent who was present at a raid six years ago.

Dwight Green: Describe your first meeting with Capone.

Chester Bragg: In May of 1925 I was with a raiding party inside a saloon on West 22nd Street.

Dwight Green: What was your role?

Chester Bragg: Well, my job was to watch the front door and keep anybody from going in or out. A big, powerful man tried to get in. I asked him, "What do you think this is, a party?" He said, "Well, it ought to be a party. I'm the owner of this place." So I said, "Come on, Al, we're waiting for you."

Dwight Green: What did the defendant do?

Chester Bragg: He went upstairs with David Morgan, another member of the raiding party. I went up later.

Dwight Green: Describe what you saw.

Chester Bragg: There were roulette wheels, pool, billiard, and crap tables.

Narrator 1: Michael Ahern, Capone's defense attorney, questions Bragg, hinting that the raid had been fixed. Then he goes too far in his questioning.

Michael Ahern: How do you have such a distinct recollection of this raid?

Chester Bragg: Well, if you had your face busted like I did, you wouldn't forget it.

Michael Ahern: You were beaten up?

Chester Bragg: Yes, as I was leaving. My nose was broken.

Narrator 2: The next witness is David Morgan. The defense attorneys try to demonstrate that Bragg hadn't gotten beaten up. However, Morgan reports being beaten as well.

The prize witness for the prosecution is Leslie Shumway, a bookkeeper for Capone's organization. Jacob Grossman, prosecuting attorney, questions Shumway.

Jacob Grossman: What kind of an establishment was the Hawthorne Smoke Shop?

Leslie Shumway: You could bet on the horses and they had a wheel, craps, 21. It was a complete establishment.

Jacob Grossman: Had you seen Capone on the premises?

Leslie Shumway: Yes, in the offices.

Jacob Grossman: How many places did you operate in?

Leslie Shumway: Five or six in the immediate neighborhood.

Jacob Grossman: Where was the money kept?

Leslie Shumway: The money was kept in a big safe in a nearby vacant building.

Narrator 1: On the second day of the trial, the prosecution enters into evidence the transcript from Capone's testimony in April 1930—when he thought he had gotten immunity in exchange for admitting that he might owe the government some money.

Narrator 2: During the week, the prosecutors demonstrate that Capone lives luxuriously and spends extravagantly. Even his phone bills and wardrobe expenditures are entered into evidence. Their primary goal is to show that Capone's expenditures prove that his income is considerably more than he reports.

Narrator 1: A key witness is Fred Ries, the gambling cashier, who previously implicated Capone.

Jacob Grossman: Mr. Ries, did you operate a gambling parlor called the Radio?

Fred Ries: Yes.

Jacob Grossman: Did you see the defendant Capone at that place in 1927?

Fred Ries: Yes, I was taking bets at the counter and he would say hello to me.

Jacob Grossman: As cashier, you had charge of the finances there, yes?

Fred Ries: Yes, sir.

Jacob Grossman: What would you do with the profits?

Fred Ries: I would buy cashier's checks. They would be turned over to Jack Guzik.

Grossman: I show you here forty-three cashier's checks. Tell us about them.

Fred Ries: They represent profits above the bankroll of $10,000 we always kept and above the expenses.

Narrator 2: The checks total $177,500 for 1927, and the prosecution then shows that Capone endorsed a check for $2,500. After demonstrating that Capone has benefited from the gambling center, the government suddenly rests its case.

Scene 8

Narrator 1: The defense is not prepared for the seemingly abrupt finish by the prosecution. Albert Fink, attorney for the defense, pleads with Judge Wilkerson.

Albert Fink: Your Honor, this is a surprise. We would like a little time to get ready for our defense.

James Herbert Wilkerson: We will discuss this shortly. Meanwhile, members of the jury, you are excused for the day.

Narrator 2: The defense attorneys complain about the prosecution's unexpected close to its case.

James Herbert Wilkerson: We have a jury confined here. I'll give you until morning.

Albert Fink: If Your Honor thinks this is fair, I'll be here. If we offer no evidence, how much time may we have for arguments?

James Herbert Wilkerson: Ten hours. Court adjourned.

Narrator 1: On Wednesday, October 14th, Albert Fink calls a defense witness, Milton Held, who is a bookie. The defense tries to demonstrate that Capone didn't profit from his activities.

Albert Fink: Have you had any transactions with the defendant?

Milton Held: Yes, I took bets from him in 1924 and 1925.

Albert Fink: Did he win?

Milton Held: He lost about $12,000.

Narrator 2: Dwight Green, a prosecuting attorney, cross-examines Held.

Dwight Green: How did you arrive at the figure of $12,000?

Milton Held: That was just an estimate.

Dwight Green: How much did Capone bet at a time?

Milton Held: Three or four hundred dollars.

Dwight Green: Did he have much money when he paid you?

Milton Held: He usually had a lot of money, mostly in $100 bills. Sometimes in $500 bills.

Narrator 1: Green then draws out the fact that Held met with Capone and his attorneys to discuss his testimony. The attorneys spend the rest of that day and the next questioning bookies who claim that Capone regularly lost money. One witness is Budd Gentry, who worked at Hialeah, a horse track in Miami.

Albert Fink: What was the highest amount the defendant ever bet?

Budd Gentry: The highest he bet was $10,000 on one horse. There were several $10,000 bets.

Albert Fink: Was he a winner or a loser at the end of the season?

Budd Gentry: He lost about $100,000.

Albert Fink: Did you ever see the defendant play poker?

Budd Gentry: Yes, I played with him and the other players.

Albert Fink: Can you recall their names?

Budd Gentry: There were lots of people there. I can't recall their names. *(pausing)* I'm trying to concentrate . . .

Narrator 2: Dwight Green, a prosecuting attorney, probes Gentry's faulty memory.

Dwight Green: What were the names of the horses the defendant bet $10,000 on?

Budd Gentry: I don't remember.

James Herbert Wilkerson: Can you give us the name of just *one* horse?

Budd Gentry: I just can't.

Narrator 1: The defense team rests its case, neglecting to emphasize that until 1927 earnings from illegitimate activities were not taxable. They also neglect to describe the immunity deal the government previously offered.

Scene 9

Narrator 2: The prosecution begins its closing arguments with Jacob Grossman, who reviews the government's case. Then he attacks the defense's case.

Jacob Grossman: The defense witnesses showed that Capone got enough revenue to afford to lose large sums in bets. His losses totaled $217,000. Where did he get this money? He lives on a fine estate in Florida, spending money freely. We've heard of jewels and fine furnishings, all bought with cash. . . . Everything is cash with Capone.

Narrator 1: After more closing arguments from the prosecuting attorneys, the defense begins by questioning the government's motives for prosecuting Capone.

Michael Ahern: The government has sought to convict this man merely because his name is Al Capone. Why do they seek conviction on this meager evidence? Because he is the mythical Robin Hood you read so much about in all the newspapers. The evidence produced here discloses only one thing: that the defendant was extravagant. The government has spent thousands in the investigation and prosecution of this case when it might better have spent that money for soup kitchens. If you convict on this evidence, every spendthrift in the country should be imprisoned.

Narrator 2: Fink continues the summation for the defense.

Albert Fink: Capone has always intended to pay his income tax. Capone is not a piker. If he owed a tax, you may be sure his motive in not paying was not because he intended to defraud the government. The government has proved nothing. We don't know what his losses were. Is the government using this case as a way to stow Al Capone away? If this defendant's name were not Al Capone, there would be no case. You would be laughing at this so-called evidence.

Narrator 1: Finally, George E. Q. Johnson wraps up the summation for the prosecution.

George E. Q. Johnson: Every morning thousands of men and women go to their daily work and every one of those workers must pay income tax. The government has no more important function, except during war, than to enforce the revenue laws of this country. If the time comes when the American people pay taxes only when the government investigates to determine their tax, then government will fail. The army and the navy will disband, and our institutions will disappear. Our courts will be swept aside. American civilization will fail, and organized society will revert to the days of the jungle, where every man will be for himself.

Narrator 2: Johnson then turns his attention directly to Capone.

George E. Q. Johnson: I have been a little bewildered at how the defense has attempted to weave a halo of mystery and romance around this man. Who is this man who has so lavishly spent almost half a million dollars? Has he found a pot of gold at the end of the rainbow? Or is he Robin Hood, as his attorney has said? Did Capone spend lavishly on the wardrobes of the needy? No.

Narrator 1: Johnson then reviews the government's witnesses, emphasizing how they demonstrate that Capone has evaded paying taxes. Then he asks a key question.

George E. Q. Johnson: At any time, at any place, has this defendant ever appeared in a reputable business? Have there appeared any records such those as honest citizens keep? The government asks you not to take a single fact. We ask you to take the whole picture. When you do that, you will find that every page of this record cries out the guilt of this defendant. Think about the thousands of men and women who go to work and pay their taxes. This is a case future generations will remember because it will establish whether any man can escape the burdens of the government.

Narrator 2: Judge Wilkerson explains in his instructions to the jury that the evidence of Capone's spending in Chicago and Miami are sufficient to demonstrate that he had considerable income.

James Herbert Wilkerson: You are the judges of the weight that is to be given to the testimony of the witnesses in this case. You should weigh the testimony calmly and dispassionately, and then reach a conclusion as to its relevance to the case.

Narrator 1: And now, you the audience must weigh the facts as you have heard them. Is Alphonse Capone guilty of income tax evasion?

Scene 10

Narrator 2: The jury takes as many as twenty ballots. All but one juror want to convict Capone on all counts. The lone holdout argues that they should temper the verdict. After nine hours, the jury returns to the courtroom.

James Herbert Wilkerson: Have you arrived at a verdict?

Foreman: We have, Your Honor. On indictment No. 22852, we find the defendant not guilty.

Narrator 1: This indictment refers to Capone's failure to pay taxes for 1924.

Foreman: On indictment No. 23232, we find the defendant guilty on counts 1, 5, 9, 13, and 18.

Narrator 2: Capone has been found guilty for the years 1925 through 1929, with three felonies and two misdemeanors. He is found not guilty on several other counts. The guilty verdicts carry heavy financial penalties and possible imprisonment.

Narrator 1: Capone and his attorneys are not surprised, assuming he'll be fined and have up to five years in jail. On October 24th, Capone returns to court to hear Wilkerson's sentence.

James Herbert Wilkerson: It is the judgment of this court that on count 1 the defendant is sentenced to imprisonment in a penitentiary for a period of five years, and to pay a fine of $10,000 and all costs of prosecution.

Narrator 2: This is essentially what Capone expects. He appears calm and relatively relaxed.

James Herbert Wilkerson: On count 5, the defendant is sentenced to five years in a penitentiary and to pay a fine of $10,000 and all costs of prosecution. On count 9 the defendant is sentenced to five years in a penitentiary and pay a fine of $10,000 and all costs of prosecution.

Narrator 1: For the misdemeanors, Capone is ordered to receive two years in a county jail and pay $10,000. Capone looks increasingly worried, wondering if he will serve the terms consecutively instead of concurrently. The judge delivers his ruling—$80,00 in fines, ten years in a federal penitentiary, and one year in a county jail.

Narrator 2: Capone struggles to remain calm. His attorneys ask for time to file appeals before Capone is sent to a federal penitentiary. All appeals fail.

Narrator 1: Capone is transferred from Cook County Prison to Atlanta Federal Penitentiary, where he becomes convict number 40886. He later goes to Alcatraz, where there are many attempts on his life.

Narrator 2: Capone's health begins to deteriorate and he is unable to continue his involvement in gangland politics. He serves out his sentence until he is released in November 1939. His family takes him to his Florida mansion, and they care for him until his death of a stroke on January 25, 1947.

10

When the Bough Breaks

The State vs. Hauptmann
The Trial of Bruno Richard Hauptmann
for the Kidnapping and Murder of
Charles A. Lindbergh, Jr.

Bruno Richard Hauptmann, *extreme right, facing forward,* defendant for the kidnapping and murder of the son of **Charles A. Lindbergh**. AP Photo.

INTRODUCTION

In 1932, the nation was horrified to learn that Charles A. Lindbergh Jr., the twenty-month-old son of one of the most popular public families in the United States, had disappeared. Colonel Charles A. Lindbergh was known for his flying exploits, especially his solo flight from New York to Paris in 1927. His wife, Anne Morrow Lindbergh, was a poet and writer, and the daughter of the late Senator Dwight W. Morrow. The couple, considered by many to be the "first family of America," divided their time between the Morrow home in Englewood, New Jersey, and their secluded, weekend retreat in Hopewell, New Jersey. On March 1, the fateful day of the child's kidnapping, the family had deviated from their planned return to the Morrow home because the child had a cold. That evening, someone leaned a ladder against the house, entered the child's bedroom, and took the child away. By the next morning, hundreds of members of the press had converged upon the Hopewell home. The investigation dragged on for years, and the American people were anxious for resolution. The trial of alleged kidnapper, Bruno Richard Hauptmann was one of the most sensational in U.S. history.

PRESENTATION SUGGESTIONS

The following characters have primary roles and should sit onstage throughout the play: David T. Wilentz, Edward J. Reilly, Thomas W. Trenchard, and Richard Bruno Hauptmann. The other characters can wait offstage or on chairs at the sides of the stage. Witnesses and attorneys for the prosecution can stand or sit on one side, with witnesses and attorneys for the defense on the other side. David T. Wilentz, Edward J. Reilly, and Anthony M. Hauck have long passages. Readers should have ample time to practice reading aloud these passages. Students can research the dress of the period and prepare appropriate costumes. If time is limited, consider dividing this script into two parts, with the second part beginning with Scene 8.

RELATED BOOKS

Fisher, Jim. *The Ghosts of Hopewell: Setting the Record Straight in the Lindbergh Case.* Carbondale, IL: Southern Illinois University Press, 1999.

Kraft, Betsy Harvey. *Sensational Trials of the 20th Century.* New York: Scholastic, 1998.

Whipple, Sidney B. *The Trial of Bruno Richard Hauptmann.* Garden City, NY: Doubleday, Doran and Company, 1937.

THE STATE VS. HAUPTMANN

CHARACTERS

Narrator 1

David T. Wilentz, *Attorney General and prosecuting attorney*

Edward J. Reilly, *defense attorney*

Thomas W. Trenchard, *presiding judge*

Narrator 2

Anne Morrow Lindbergh, *mother of the murdered child*

Colonel Charles A. Lindbergh, *father of the murdered child and famous aviator*

Betsy Mowat Gow, *nursemaid*

Lewis J. Bornmann, *state police officer*

Amandus Hochmuth, *elderly neighbor and witness*

John F. Condon, *lecturer at Fordham University and liaison to the kidnapper*

John Joseph Lyons, *gas station attendant and witness*

C. Lloyd Fisher, *defense attorney*

Richard Bruno Hauptmann, *the defendant: alleged kidnapper and murderer*

Anna Hauptmann, *wife of Richard Bruno Hauptmann*

John M. Trendley, *handwriting expert for the defense*

Anthony M. Hauck, *prosecuting attorney*

When the Bough Breaks

The State vs. Hauptmann
The Trial of Bruno Richard Hauptmann
for the Kidnapping and Murder of
Charles A. Lindbergh, Jr.

Scene 1

Narrator 1: At ten o'clock on the morning on the third day of January, 1935, eager spectators and reporters fill the courtroom in Flemington, New Jersey. After nearly three years of investigation, the trial of Bruno Richard Hauptman, the alleged kidnapper and murderer of young Charles A. Lindbergh, Jr., is beginning. Because of the fame of the child's parents, the abduction and investigation have received intense attention from the public and the press. Twelve jury members listen to Attorney General David T. Wilentz's opening statement.

David T. Wilentz: May it please Your Honor, Mr. Foreman, men and women of the jury: A grand jury has found that Charles A. Lindbergh, Jr., just twenty months old, was kidnapped and murdered on the night of March 1st, 1932, from the Lindbergh's home in Hopewell, New Jersey. The Lindbergh household consisted of Betty Gow, Oliver and Elsie Whatley, Colonel Charles A. Lindbergh, his wife, and their only son, Charles Junior.

We will prove to you that the man who plotted the crime sits in this very courtroom. Bruno Richard Hauptmann brought a ladder to the house, entered the child's second-floor bedroom through a window, and left with the child. Weighed down with the child, the ladder broke—and the child died in the fall. Having no use for the ladder or the child, he first abandoned the ladder. Then, he ripped the sleeping garment off the child, and, a few miles away, scooped up a hastily improvised and shallow grave and put this child in face downwards. Then he went on his way.

You'll hear about the Lindberghs' desperate search for their child, the discovery of the ransom note, and how $50,000 was exchanged by a trusted intermediary, John Condon, for a note telling where to find the baby in Bay Head, Massachusetts. The search for the baby was fruitless and the child remained missing until May 12, 1932, when a gentleman, driving along the highway, got off the beaten path of the road and into a woods to answer the call of nature—and there found the body of an infant. That child was Charles A. Lindbergh, Jr.

For nearly two years, investigators had no success in finding the kidnapper. Then Bruno Richard Hauptmann was caught using a numbered, ten-dollar gold note that was part of the ransom money. When Hauptmann was arrested, what did investigators find?

They discovered that Hauptmann had another numbered bill in his wallet. They found John Condon's telephone number and address written on an inside closet wall in Hauptmann's home. Parts of the ladder used in the kidnapping came from the Bronx Lumber Corporation—where Hauptmann once worked. And, one rung of that ladder came right from his attic, put on the ladder with his tools. Nearly $14,000 in cash was found hidden in Hauptmann's garage.

We'll prove to you that Hauptmann committed this crime because he wanted money—lots of money—and he got it. He wanted that money so he could live a life of luxury and ease. He quit his job the day he collected the $50,000, the very day . . .

Now, men and women of the jury, if we do not prove these facts to you, why, you acquit him. But if we do, as we are confident we will, we demand the penalty for murder in the first degree.

Edward T. Reilly: If Your Honor please, I move for a mistrial. The attorney general did not give a proper opening, but gave a summation. He intends to inflame the minds of this jury against this defendant before the trial starts.

Thomas W. Trenchard: The motion is denied.

Scene 2

Narrator 2: Mr. Wilentz begins questioning Anne Lindbergh about her activities on the day of the kidnapping, asking her to describe the bedtime preparations.

Anne Lindbergh: He wore a homemade flannel shirt that Miss Gow cut out and sewed that night out of a flannel petticoat.

David T. Wilentz: Is this the flannel shirt that your child had on that night in that crib when he was put to bed on March 1, 1932?

Anne Lindbergh: It is.

David T. Wilentz: What else did the child wear that evening?

Anne Lindbergh: He had diapers, fastened to the small shirt, to the second shirt, and on top of that he had a sleeping suit.

David T. Wilentz: Is this the sleeping suit that your son wore that night as he went to bed?

Anne Lindbergh: It is.

David T. Wilentz: Did the child have any thumb protectors on?

Anne Lindbergh: Yes, he had.

David T. Wilentz: Do you recognize this as being one of the thumb guards that was used for your child?

Anne Lindbergh: Yes.

Narrator 1: Mr. Wilentz continues to question Mrs. Lindbergh about her evening activities.

After Mr. Reilly declines the opportunity to cross-examine her, the state calls Mr. Lindbergh to the stand.

David T. Wilentz: What is your occupation?

Colonel Charles A. Lindbergh: My occupation is aviation.

David T. Wilentz: When you got home, will you tell us briefly what happened from then until about ten o'clock?

Colonel Charles A. Lindbergh: I put the car in the garage at the west end of the house. From there I went in through the kitchen and joined my wife at supper. After supper I retired to the library.

David T. Wilentz: Sometime during that night, did you hear some sort of a noise or crash?

Colonel Charles A. Lindbergh: Yes, I did . . . I heard a sound that seemed to me . . . of—well, say, an orange crate falling off a chair, which I assumed to be in the kitchen. I did not pay very much attention to it at the time, but enough to remark to my wife the words: "What is that?"

David T. Wilentz: And about what time was that?

Colonel Charles A. Lindbergh: That would be about 9:10 or 9:15.

David T. Wilentz: Was it the sort of a noise that would come with the falling of a ladder?

Colonel Charles A. Lindbergh: Yes, if the ladder was outside.

David T. Wilentz: Finally, at about ten o'clock in the evening, Miss Gow spoke to you about the child, did she not?

Colonel Charles A. Lindbergh: Miss Gow called to me in a rather excited voice and asked me if I had the baby.

David T. Wilentz: What happened from then on?

Colonel Charles A. Lindbergh: I immediately went upstairs into the nursery, where I realized that something had gone wrong.

David T. Wilentz: Did you see a note in the room?

Colonel Charles A. Lindbergh: Yes, I did . . . on the windowsill.

David T. Wilentz: I ask permission of the court to read the note.

Thomas W. Trenchard: You may read it.

Narrator 2: Mr. Wilentz reads parts of the letter aloud, noting the misspellings. The note has a distinctive three holes, accompanied by a red mark.

David T. Wilentz: Here is what the letter said. "Dear Sir: Have 50,000 dollars ready. After 2–4 days we will inform you where to deliver the money. We warn you against making anything public or for notify the police. The child is in gut [sic] care. Instruction for the letters are singnature [sic]. Then you find these two circles and . . . this red blotch . . . Singnature [sic] three holes."

Narrator 1: Wilentz continues questioning Mr. Lindbergh, who describes how he called the police and his friend and attorney, Colonel Breckinridge. While waiting for help, he took his rifle and searched the road. He testifies about the impressions in the ground outside the child's window, the general confusion during the search, followed by the arrival of several hundred members of the press before daybreak.

Narrator 2: Wilentz reads aloud the second note that arrived by mail, which warned the Lindberghs not to contact the police and to settle the matter quietly. The note contains similar misspellings and the distinctive three holes and red blotch. Wilentz guides Lindbergh through the arrangements with Dr. Condon regarding the exchange of the money and his fruitless search in his plane for the boat that promised to hold the child, as described in the final note.

David T. Wilentz: In March of 1932, when was the last time you saw Charles A. Lindbergh, Jr.?

Colonel Charles A. Lindbergh: On the Sunday evening preceding the first of March.

David T. Wilentz: Did you ever see that child alive again?

Colonel Charles A. Lindbergh: I did not.

David T. Wilentz: Did you see the child at all?

Colonel Charles A. Lindbergh: I saw the body . . .

David T. Wilentz: You did not get the money back and did not get your child?

Colonel Charles A. Lindbergh: I did not.

Scene 3

Narrator 1: After questioning Lindbergh about Lindbergh's routine, the staff, and the layout of the house, Wilentz addresses access to the house.

David T. Wilenz: Colonel, while you were in the dining room, if the front doorway of your home was opened by someone, anyone could have gone up the stairway and taken the baby out of the crib, couldn't they?

Colonel Charles A. Lindbergh: I think it would be very improbable that that could be done without our hearing it.

David T. Wilentz: Would it be possible for anyone in the house . . . to take the baby out of the crib and bring it down the main stairs? Or bring it to a window?

Colonel Charles A. Lindbergh: It might have been possible.

David T. Wilentz: The message that the baby was missing was brought to you by Miss Gow?

Colonel Charles A. Lindbergh: Yes.

Narrator 2: Wilentz questions Lindbergh about the staff, Mr. and Mrs. Whateley, and Betty Gow, the child's nursemaid.

David T. Wilentz: Was the window locked?

Colonel Charles A. Lindbergh: No, it wasn't the custom to lock windows.

David T. Wilentz: And was it known to the staff that the window was not locked generally.

Colonel Charles A. Lindbergh: I suppose so.

Narrator 1: Wilentz questions Lindbergh about the investigation, the notes, and the preparation of ransom money. Then he focuses on Miss Violet Sharpe, a waitress employed by the Morrows. Sharpe was engaged to the Morrow butler, Septimus Banks. After intense questioning by the police, Miss Sharpe drank poison, causing the police to consider her a suspect.

David T. Wilentz: Colonel, were you in the Morrow home shortly before the suicide of Violet Sharpe?

Colonel Charles A. Lindbergh: Yes.

David T. Wilentz: Did you know that she and the butler were friendly outside of the home?

Colonel Charles A. Lindbergh: I would be surprised if they were.

David T. Wilentz: Did you suspect Violet Sharpe of any connection with the case?

Colonel Charles A. Lindbergh: I did not.

David T. Wilentz: Well, is it not a fact that she had been questioned by the state police, that they came back to ask her more questions, and that she went upstairs after their presence was announced to her and committed suicide?

Colonel Charles A. Lindbergh: She committed suicide. I do not know whether it was prior to being questioned a second time.

Scene 4

Narrator 2: Mr. Wilentz establishes that the Lindberghs had employed Bessie Gow as the nursemaid since February of 1931. He probes about the baby's cold and Miss Gow's sewing of a flannel shirt for the baby to wear that night.

David T. Wilentz: Now I show you Exhibit S-13. What is it?

Betsy Mowat Gow: This is the exact little shirt I made for the baby that night.

David T. Wilentz: Well, finally, the child was ready for bed, I take it, and you left the room?

Betsy Mowat Gow: Yes, the child was ready for bed; I put him in his bed. Mrs. Lindbergh and I went around the windows, closed the shutters. We closed all the shutters tight except the one at the southeast window. This one we couldn't quite close. It had evidently warped, so we closed it as best we could and left it that way.

David T. Wilentz: You could not lock it?

Betsy Mowat Gow: No.

Narrator 1: How did you discover that the child was missing?

Betsy Mowat Gow: I came in and found the French window was open. I closed that window, plugged in the electric heater, and stood for about one minute waiting for the room to lose its chill. I then crossed to the bed and bent over with my hands on the rail and discovered I couldn't hear the baby breathe. I bent down, felt all over for him, and discovered he wasn't there. I thought that Mrs. Lindbergh may have him. I went out of the baby's room into the hallway and into Mrs. Lindbergh's room. I met her or saw her coming out of the bathroom and asked her if she had the baby. She looked surprised and said, no, she didn't. Mr. Lindbergh checked the room again. Then he ran into his closet, came out again with a rifle and began searching the house while we waited for the police.

Narrator 2: Gow describes the discovery of the thumb guard near the gate to the premises about a month after the kidnapping, and her eventual identification of the baby's body in the morgue in Trenton. Then Mr. Reilly begins the cross-examination. He focuses on who might know that the Lindberghs were staying at the Hopewell weekend home instead of returning to the Morrow residence, as was their custom. Miss Gow, who had been at the Morrow home, had just joined the family at the Hopewell home that day.

Edward T. Reilly: Why did Mrs. Lindbergh call and ask you to come over Tuesday?

Betsy Mowat Gow: Mrs. Lindbergh called me Monday and said the baby had a slight cold.

Edward T. Reilly: Did you tell anyone that the Lindberghs were not coming back Monday night?

Betsy Mowat Gow: I probably did.

Edward T. Reilly: Why?

Betsy Mowat Gow: It was a natural thing for anyone to ask me why the baby wasn't coming back and I would reply that he had a slight cold.

Edward T. Reilly: But you told no outsiders or strangers?

Betsy Mowat Gow: No.

Narrator 1: Reilly reviews Gow's movements the night of the kidnapping and concludes his cross-examination.

Scene 5

Narrator 2: Mr. Wilentz calls Lewis J. Bornmann, a state police officer, to the stand, asking about the ladder that was found near the house.

David T. Wilentz: Is this the ladder you picked up during the search for the missing child?

Lewis J. Bornmann: Yes sir, it is.

David T. Wilentz: Three sections?

Lewis J. Bornmann: Three sections. Two were lying together, and one section about ten feet further on. One section had split. The sections had been connected with a dowel pin.

Edward T. Reilly: Did you see the butler when you came in?

Lewis J. Bornmann: No.

Edward T. Reilly: What shoe size did the butler wear?

Lewis J. Bornmann: I never questioned him as to that.

Edward T. Reilly: Everybody in the house was subject to questioning, am I correct?

Lewis J. Bornmann: Naturally, they were.

Narrator 1: During cross-examination, Reilly establishes that the officer took the butler's word that he'd not been outside and Mrs. Lindbergh's statement that she *had* been outside, probably leaving the woman's footprint that had been found.

Narrator 2: Next, the attorneys shift their attention to Frank A. Kelly, a former state police trooper, who checked the nursery and ransom note for fingerprints and handled the investigation of the ladder. He testifies that the ladder fit in the indentations in the ground and that marks near the top of the ladder correspond with marks found on the wall of the house. Then the prosecution turns its attention to Amandus Hochmuth, a resident of Hunterdon County.

David T. Wilentz: Mr. Hochmuth, tell us about your experience the morning of March 1.

Amandus Hochmuth: Well, I saw a car coming around the corner, pretty good speed, and I expected it to turn over on the ditch. The man in there glared at me as if he saw a ghost.

David T. Wilentz: And the man that you saw looking out of that automobile . . . is he in this room?

Narrator 1: Hochmuth indicates Bruno Hauptmann.

David T. Wilentz: Was there a ladder in the car?

Amandus Hochmuth: I saw something of a ladder in it.

Narrator: Reilly cross-examines.

Edward T. Reilly: Mr. Hochmuth, you say you are how old?

Amandus Hochmuth: I am in my eighty-seventh year.

Edward T. Reilly: Your health is rather poor, isn't it?

Amandus Hochmuth: It don't seem like it.

Edward T. Reilly: Well, I notice that you are shaking.

Amandus Hochmuth: I have had a good deal of rheumatism.

Edward T. Reilly: Are you nearsighted or farsighted?

Amandus Hochmuth: My eyes are all right.

Edward T. Reilly: I didn't ask that, mister. You are wearing glasses. Why do you wear glasses—to see better?

Amandus Hochmuth: At a distance, yes. For reading, I read without glasses.

Scene 6

Narrator 2: John Condon, a lecturer at Fordham University, is one of many prominent citizens who volunteered to act as a go-between after the child was kidnapped. In an interview in the *Home News,* a community paper in the Bronx, Condon urged the kidnapper to contact him. Condon subsequently communicated with the kidnapper through the personal ads in the newspaper. Wilentz now questions Condon regarding the delivery of the ransom on April 2, 1932, at St. Raymond's Cemetery.

David T. Wilentz: What happened when you got there?

John F. Condon: The man I met says, "Have you got the money?"

David T. Wilentz: What did you say?

John F. Condon: I said, "No, I didn't bring any money. It's up in the car." He said, "Who is up there?" I said, "Colonel Lindbergh."

David T. Wilentz: Then what?

John F. Condon: He told me to get the money, but I told him I'd need something showing where the baby is. He said he would get a note. I returned to the car. Lindbergh handed approximately $50,000 to me, which I exchanged for the note.

David T. Wilentz: And that man you handed that money to was called John, you say.

John F. Condon: John.

David T. Wilentz: And John is who?

John F. Condon: John is Bruno Richard Hauptmann.

Narrator 1: Condon describes the misspellings on the note, which said that the boy was on the "boad *Nelly*" with two people on board. The note said that the boat was near Elizabeth Island. Condon testifies how Lindbergh and his associates left for Connecticut and began searching near Gay Head. The trial continues with testimony from handwriting experts who state that the ransom notes are consistent with handwriting samples obtained from Hauptmann. Testimony follows from the man who discovered the body of the child in a hollow in the woods at Mount Rose Hill, New Jersey. The Mercer County physician describes the cause of death—a fractured skull.

Scene 7

Narrator 2: Employees of J.P. Morgan and Company had prepared the ransom money, recording the numbers of the ten-dollar gold certificates. John Joseph Lyons, a gas station station attendant now testifies.

David T. Wilentz: Did you see Bruno Richard Hauptmann sometime in 1934?

John Joseph Lyons: Yes, at ten o'clock in the morning, September 15th. A dark Dodge sedan pulled in on the station and pulled to an ethyl pump. Mr. Lyle, the manager, served him five gallons of gas.

David T. Wilentz: Did Mr. Lyle get money for five gallons of gas?

John Joseph Lyons: Yes sir. A ten-dollar gold certificate.

David T. Wilentz: Did you have any more conversation?

John Joseph Lyons: Lyle said, "You don't see many more of them."

David T. Wilentz: What did Hauptmann say?

John Joseph Lyons: He said, "I only got a hundred more left."

David T. Wilentz: What happened then?

John Joseph Lyons: Lyle gave him the change and Hauptmann got in the car and went away. We walked in the office and Lyle wrote the license plate number down on the ten-dollar gold certificate.

Narrator 1: After the bill is accepted as evidence, William F. Seery, special agent for the Division of Investigation, U.S. Department of Justice, testifies how the bill and license plate led to Hauptmann. He describes how Hauptmann had a twenty-dollar gold bill when arrested. Seery testifies that Hauptmann, upon questioning, claimed that over a period of years he had been assembling gold certificates, fearing inflation. Seery describes the search of Hauptmann's house and garage and the discovery of approximately $14,000 in gold certificates in Hauptmann's garage.

Narrator 2: A New York City police detective, Maurice W. Tobin, then recounts the discovery of a board in a closet on which was written John Condon's address and telephone number. Another detective, Lewis J. Bornmann, describes how the sixteenth rail of the ladder is a perfect fit for a missing attic floorboard. Saw marks and nail holes also match. At the conclusion of extensive testimony and cross-examination about the board and nail holes, the State rests its case.

Scene 8

Narrator 1: Mr. Egbert Rosecrans, defense attorney, begins by moving for acquittal based on the lack of evidence regarding the actual location of the child's death. He emphasizes that the sole witness to Mr. Hauptmann's presence near Hopewell is an elderly gentleman who testified he saw the defendant upon the morning of the crime. After rebuttal by Mr. Wilentz, the judge denies the request. Defense attorney C. Lloyd Fisher offers a brief opening statement.

C. Lloyd Fisher: We submit that in our defense we will prove to you a complete alibi for the defendant Hauptmann on the night of the kidnapping. We will show that he went from his job to his Bronx home on 222nd Street. Then, he went to the bakery shop owned by the Fredericksens. As to the handwriting—well, we don't have the funds to bring in eight or nine expert witnesses. We *will* prove that Bruno Hauptmann did buy and sell on the market and that he traded in furs and pelts. We will prove that his businesses were profitable. You will learn that the police mishandled the evidence, adding their own fingerprints to the ladder and how they coerced Mr. Hauptmann into misspelling words when taking the handwriting samples.

We will submit this case to you as honestly and fairly as we know how. Again may I say we will be terribly handicapped by a total lack of funds. Now, we will rely on you to consider all the facts and circumstances and acquit this man of the crime with which he is charged. Thank you.

Narrator 2: Mr. Reilly calls the defendant, Bruno Hauptmann, to the stand. After establishing his date of birth and background, Mr. Reilly asks about Hauptmann's conviction in Germany.

Edward T. Reilly: Were you able to get any work after you served in the war?

Richard Bruno Hauptmann: No.

Edward T. Reilly: During the period of reconstruction in Germany, about 1919 and 1920, you were convicted of some offense there. Is that correct?

Richard Bruno Hauptmann: Yes.

Edward T. Reilly: Did you serve any sentence as a result of that?

Richard Bruno Hauptmann: Yes.

Edward T. Reilly: And afterwards were you paroled?

Richard Bruno Hauptmann: Yes.

Narrator 1: Hauptmann describes how he repeatedly came to the United States as a stowaway, succeeding on his third attempt. He worked at various jobs, from dishwasher to carpenter. He met Anna Schoeffler in 1924, marrying her in 1925. Hauptmann worked as a carpenter, making about fifty dollars per week.

Edward T. Reilly: Were you spending all the money you made, or were you saving it?

Richard Bruno Hauptmann: I spent very little.

Edward T. Reilly: Did you open a bank account at any time or did you keep the cash with you?

Richard Bruno Hauptmann: I opened right in the beginning a bank account.

Edward T. Reilly: Did you keep some money in the house?

Richard Bruno Hauptmann: Yes, always. That is a habit I have.

Edward T. Reilly: You were a partner with Isidor Fisch in a fur business. What was the largest sum you received as your share in any one year?

Richard Bruno Hauptmann: I guess the largest sum was over a thousand dollars.

Edward T. Reilly: Before Fisch went to Europe, did he call at your house?

Richard Bruno Hauptmann: He called several times.

Edward T. Reilly: Before he left, did he leave anything with you to take care of?

Richard Bruno Hauptmann: Two suitcases, four hundred Hudson seal skins, and a little box.

Edward T. Reilly: What did you do with the box?

Richard Bruno Hauptmann: I put it in the broom closet. On the upper shelf.

Edward T. Reilly: How long did that shoe box remain there before you disturbed it?

Richard Bruno Hauptmann: Until the middle of August 1934.

Edward T. Reilly: Why did you disturb it?

Richard Bruno Hauptmann: I was looking for a broom. When I took the broom I must have hit the box. I looked up and saw that it was gold certificates.

Edward T. Reilly: Is that the money you started to spend?

Richard Bruno Hauptmann: Yes, that is the money. By this time I had learned that Fisch had died in Europe.

Edward T. Reilly: Hauptmann, were you ever in Hopewell?

Richard Bruno Hauptmann: I never was.

Edward T. Reilly: On the night of March 1, 1932, did you enter the nursery of Colonel Lindbergh and take from that nursery Charles Lindbergh, Jr.?

Richard Bruno Hauptmann: I did not.

Edward T. Reilly: Now, I want you to look at the State's Exhibits 17 and 18. Did you ever see that envelope and note before?

Richard Bruno Hauptmann: The first time I saw that was in the courtroom.

Narrator 2: Hauptmann describes his movements on March 1, 1932: driving his wife to the bakery where she worked, then spending the day going to various employment agencies in Manhattan. He relates how he returned home and then went to the bakery until after nine o'clock. He denies that he sent the ransom notes or met with Dr. Condon. Reilly then questions Hauptmann about the ladder.

Edward T. Reilly: Did you build the ladder?

Richard Bruno Hauptmann: Certainly not.

Edward T. Reilly: Did you take a board from your attic to use in this ladder?

Richard Bruno Hauptmann: I did not.

Edward T. Reilly: On April 2, 1932, were you in St. Raymond's Cemetery and did you receive $50,000 from Doctor Condon?

Richard Bruno Hauptmann: I did not.

Edward T. Reilly: Did you go out at any time that night?

Richard Bruno Hauptmann: We had a musical gathering at our house. I went out about 11:30 to bring a guest to the streetcar.

Narrator 1: Reilly returns to questions about the money found in the closet.

Edward T. Reilly: Did you owe Fisch, or did he owe you anything when he went to Europe?

Richard Bruno Hauptmann: I gave him $2,000 cash for his trip.

Edward T. Reilly: What did you do with the money from the box in the closet?

Richard Bruno Hauptmann: I spent some of it.

Narrator 2: Reilly continues to elicit testimony about the Hauptmann's financial circumstances. Then he addresses the arrest, the discovery of the money, and the prolonged questioning by police. Hauptmann insists that the police beat him, denied him food, and forced him to misspell words during prolonged periods of being forced to produce writing samples.

Scene 9

Narrator 1: The prosecutor begins his cross-examination of the defendant. Mr. Wilentz explores Hauptmann's illegal entry into the United States and Hauptmann's assertion that he had only been convicted once of a crime. Hauptmann admits to once having escaped jail. Then Wilentz leads Hauptmann to admit that he was convicted of breaking and entering in 1919 and using a gun while holding up two women wheeling baby carriages.

David T. Wilentz: You have been planning to go back to Germany, haven't you?

Richard Bruno Hauptmann: I was planning to go back to Germany this year.

David T. Wilentz: Just about then you were arrested, isn't that right?

Richard Bruno Hauptmann: Just about . . .

Narrator 2: Wilentz shows Hauptmann a notebook and establishes that it contained Hauptmann's handwriting.

David T. Wilentz: Now, tell me, how do you spell "boat"?

Richard Bruno Hauptmann: B-o-a-t.

David T. Wilentz: Why did you spell it b-o-a-d?

Richard Bruno Hauptmann: This is eight years old. I have made improvements in my writing.

David T. Wilentz: So at one time you spelled "boat" b-o-a-d?

Richard Bruno Hauptmann: No, I don't think so.

David T. Wilentz: You spelled it in there, didn't you?

Richard Bruno Hauptmann: I can't remember putting this in the book.

David T. Wilentz: Is the whole page in your handwriting?

Richard Bruno Hauptmann: I don't know.

David T. Wilentz: You know you wrote "boad" when you got the fifty thousand from Condon. Isn't that right?

Richard Bruno Hauptmann: No sir.

Narrator 1: Wilentz then questions Hauptmann about the money that was hidden from his wife.

David T. Wilentz: When you found $14,000, how did you feel?

Richard Bruno Hauptmann: I was excited.

David T. Wilentz: Did you say anything, like, "Anna, look what I found!"?

Richard Bruno Hauptmann: No, I did not.

David T. Wilentz: She gave you every dollar she had in the world didn't she?

Richard Bruno Hauptmann: So did I.

David T. Wilentz: Except these $14,000.

Richard Bruno Hauptmann: Why should I make my wife excited about it?

Narrator 2: After extensive questioning about the Hauptmanns' financial situation, Wilentz turns to the matter of Dr. Condon's phone number recorded on the board inside the closet. At first Hauptmann claims to have never written on the board. Then he admits that when he was originally questioned he said that he might have written the address and phone number on the board because he reads the paper in the closet and likes to write down details of interest. Hauptmann asserts that he changed his responses to questioning because of the extensive questions and mistreatment by the police during his initial questioning.

Scene 10

Narrator 1: After questioning Mrs. Hauptmann about her immigration to the United States, her job at the Fredericksen's bakery, and her husband's relationship with

THE STATE VS. HAUPTMANN

Mr. Fisch, Mr. Reilly questions her about the box of money kept on the closet shelf. Mrs. Hauptmann asserts that she can't reach that shelf and has no occasion to look on the shelf. Then the cross-examination begins.

David T. Wilentz: You never saw a shoebox in the closet?

Anna Hauptmann: I didn't.

David T. Wilentz: Take a look at this picture of the closet. Is that a correct picture of the closet?

Anna Hauptmann: This is the closet here.

David T. Wilentz: Take a look at the apron on the hook. Is that where the hook was when you were living there?

Anna Hauptmann: I believe so.

David T. Wilentz: You used to take your apron and hang it up there, didn't you?

Anna Hauptmann: Oh, I could hang it up.

David T. Wilentz: That hook is above the top shelf of the closet. You had no trouble reaching above the top shelf of the closet to hang your apron.

Anna Hauptmann: I had no trouble reaching it.

David T. Wilentz: And you know if you stood a few feet away from it you could see everything on that top shelf?

Anna Hauptmann: Why should I stay away a few feet and look up there?

Narrator 2: The two continue arguing this point, with Mrs. Hauptmann insisting she had no need to look on the top shelf. Mrs. Hauptmann also insists that she never noticed the box when cleaning the closet. Final testimony demonstrates how unused nail holes on a rung of the ladder matched those found in joists in the Hauptmann's attic, leading to the conclusion that the board was originally in the attic.

Narrator 1: Next, Mr. Reilly questions John M. Trendley, a handwriting expert.

Edward J. Reilly: Now, Mr. Trendley, you have given a great deal of thought to this case, haven't you?

John M. Trendley: I should say I have.

Edward J. Reilly: In fact, you volunteered your services in this case, didn't you?

John M. Trendley: I did.

Edward J. Reilly: Did you find any words in the ransom note that matched Mr. Hauptman's handwriting?

John M. Trendley: In the ten lines I examined, only one word matched.

Edward J. Reilly: What word is that?

John M. Trendley: The word *is*.

Edward J. Reilly: In your opinion would that be sufficient to send a man to the electric chair?

David T. Wilentz: Objection.

Thomas W. Trenchard: Sustained.

John M. Trendley: Yes. In examining all the ransom notes, I think there were something like over three hundred letter *a*'s and I find all through the *a*'s it is a round form entirely. In all of the requested writings from the defendant I find the *a*'s of the oval form, in which the height exceeded the width. Now my contention would be that no man—it would be humanly impossible, no matter how skillful a writer you were, to write fourteen letters at fourteen different intervals without injecting some of your characteristics. It's an unconscious movement, a nervous reflex, and is independent of the writer's own will, and I would expect to find over half of his characteristics in those ransom notes if Hauptmann ever penned a line in it.

Edward J. Reilly: Please discuss your findings with regards to the letter k.

John M. Trendley: I never found a "k" of Hauptmann's style of writing in the requested samples. He never deviated from his own handwriting. I think that is the most outstanding characteristic in this whole case of the ransom letters. If Hauptmann wrote those letters, he would have to disguise all his letters and he couldn't keep all those letters in his mind while he was writing.

Scene 11

Narrator 1: Mr. Hauck provides the summation for the prosecution.

Anthony M. Hauck: May it please the court, ladies and gentlemen of the jury . . . the state of New Jersey contends that they have proven conclusively that Bruno Richard Hauptmann is guilty of murder in the first degree. We have proven that the baby was removed from the nursery. The ladder broke as the kidnapper left, carrying the child. You have heard that the child died from a fractured skull caused by a severe blow. We have proven that a witness saw Hauptmann in the area on March 1st, that a board from Hauptmann's attic was part of the ladder, and that Hauptmann's handwriting matched that found on the ransom notes. Then we have Doctor Condon, the man who said that he handed Bruno Richard Hauptmann $50,000 of Colonel Lindbergh's money. We have shown you conclusively, overwhelmingly, beyond a reasonable doubt, that Bruno Richard Hauptmann is guilty of the murder of Charles A. Lindbergh, Jr.

Narrator 2: Mr. Reilly begins his summation in defense of Hauptmann.

Edward T. Reilly: May it please Your Honor . . . ladies and gentlemen of the jury . . . Now they would have you believe that this man Hauptmann was a mastermind, that he planned this complex crime himself. The first thing you have to decide when you go into your jury room is how Hauptmann knew anything about the Lindbergh home. How would a man who lives seventy-five miles away know enough about the home and habits of the Lindberghs to kidnap the child? A man can't come up to a strange house with a ladder and stack it up against the wall, run up the ladder, walk into a room that he has never been in before, and leave with a child. Yet that is what the prosecutors would have you believe.

Now, I ask the mothers on the jury to think about this. The moment anyone put their hand on that child, that child's cry would have brought the mother from the room across the hall. The person who picked that child out of that crib knew that child, and that child knew that person. Fingerprints weren't found anywhere. Who rubbed them out? As for the handwriting, the experts were giving their *opinion* about the handwriting. You heard Mr. Trendley testify that a man couldn't sustain that sort of consistency, especially after two years. Even if you want to accept the other testimony, is there sufficient certainty regarding the handwriting to send a man to his death?

And about Dr. Condon's role in this charade. Why did he get involved in this? Who saw him hand over the $50,000? That graveyard should have been surrounded by police.

As for Violet Sharpe, a girl as sophisticated as her doesn't commit suicide just because she fears she might lose her job. Someone with nothing to hide doesn't swallow cyanide of potassium.

The prosecution has not begun to address the issue of the remaining ransom money. Where is the remaining $35,000? In spite of the lack of evidence, my client was subjected to hours of brutal questioning, which included being forced to duplicate the ransom notes. The prosecution would have you believe a man, who never had a telephone in his life, crawled into a dark closet and wrote Dr. Condon's telephone number on it. This is the worst example of police crookedness that I have seen in a great many years. As for the ladder . . . I only hope there are some carpenters on the jury because a carpenter, especially a skilled carpenter such as Mr. Hauptmann, never made this ladder.

I believe this man is absolutely innocent of murder. And I feel sure, in closing, even Colonel Lindbergh wouldn't expect you to do anything but your duty under the law.

Narrator 1: Mr. Wilentz begins the final summation by highlighting the testimony of the handwriting experts and of Betty Gow, and points out that not one single ransom dollar was ever traced to anybody connected with any member of the household.

David T. Wilentz: Let me tell you this: Hauptmann took no chance on the child awakening. He crushed that child right in that room. He smothered and choked that child right there in that room. He wasn't interested in the child. Life meant nothing to him. Public Enemy Number 1 of the world! That's what we are dealing with! It seems to me that you will have the courage if you are convinced, as all of us are—the federal authorities, the Bronx people who were there, the New Jersey State Police, the lawyers, Colonel Lindbergh, everybody who has testified—if you believe with us, you have got to find him guilty of murder in the first degree.

Narrator 2: Judge Trenchard gives instructions to jury, emphasizing the meaning of "reasonable doubt."

Thomas W. Trenchard: Reasonable doubt is not a mere possible doubt, because everything relating to human affairs is open to some doubt. It is that state of the case, which, after consideration of all the evidence, leaves the minds of the jurors so that they cannot say that they feel conviction to a certainty.

Narrator 1: Trenchard then reviews the key positions of both sides before closing his instructions.

Thomas W. Trenchard: If you find that the murder was committed by the defendant in perpetrating a burglary, it is murder in the first degree, even though the killing was unintentional . . . If you find the defendant guilty of murder in the first degree, you may, if you see fit, recommend imprisonment at hard labor for life. If you should return a verdict of murder in the first degree and nothing else, the punishment would be death.

Narrator 2: And now, you the audience must weigh the facts as you have heard them. As in all murder trials, you must all agree upon your verdict. Did Bruno Richard Hauptmann kidnap and kill Charles A. Lindbergh, Jr.?

Scene 12

Narrator 1: After less than eleven hours of deliberations on February 13, 1935, Bruno Richard Hauptmann was found guilty of murder, without recommendation for mercy. An appeal was denied in October 1935. A stay of execution was granted pending appeal to the United States Supreme Court, which refused to intervene as of December 9, 1935. After thirty-day and forty-eight-hour reprieves, Hauptmann, who always maintained his innocence was electrocuted on April 3, 1936. His wife, Anna, continued to assert his innocence for six decades. She died at the age of 95 on October 10, 1994, the sixty-ninth anniversary of her marriage.

Bibliography

Asinof, Eliot. *Eight Men Out: The Black Sox and the 1919 World Series.* New York: Henry Holt, 1987.

Bergreen, Lawrence. *Al Capone: The Man and the Era.* New York: Simon and Schuster, 1994.

Blake, Arthur. *The Scopes Trial: Defending the Right to Teach.* Brookfield, CT: Millbrook Press, 1994.

Caudill, Edward. *The Scopes Trial: A Photographic History.* Knoxville, TN: The University of Tennessee Press, 2000.

Darrow, Clarence. *The Story of My Life.* New York: Charles Scribner's Sons, 1932.

———. *Verdicts Out of Court.* Chicago: Quadrangle Books, 1963.

Fisher, Jim. *The Ghosts of Hopewell: Setting the Record Straight in the Lindbergh Case.* Carbondale, IL: Southern Illinois University Press, 1999.

Geis, Gilbert and Leigh B. Bienen. *Crimes of the Century.* Boston: Northeastern University Press, 1998.

Grant, Robert, and Joseph Katz. *The Great Trials of the Twenties: The Watershed Decade in America's Courtrooms.* Rockville Centre, NY: Sarpedon, 1998.

Hanchett, William. *The Lincoln Murder Conspiracies.* Urbana and Chicago: University of Illinois Press, 1983.

Kendall, Martha E. *Susan B. Anthony: Voice for Women's Voting Rights.* Berkeley Heights, NJ: Enslow Publishing, 1997.

King, David C. *Al Capone and the Roaring Twenties.* Farmington Hills, MI: The Gale Group, 1998.

Kraft, Betsy Harvey. *Sensational Trials of the 20th Century.* New York: Scholastic, 1998.

Lutholtz, William M. *Grand Dragon: D.C. Stephenson and the Ku Klux Klan in Indiana.* West Lafeyette, IN: Purdue University Press, 1991.

MacDonald, Alan. *Al and His Gang.* New York: Scholastic, 2000.

Monroe, Judy. *The Susan B. Anthony Women's Voting Rights Trial: A Headline Court Case.* Berkeley Heights, NJ: Enslow Publishing, 2002.

Rappaport, Doreen. *The Lizzie Borden Trial.* New York: HarperCollins, 1992. Grades 4–7.

Rebello, Leonard. *Lizzie Borden Past and Present.* Fall River, MA: Al-Zach Press, 1999.

Schuetz, Janice. *The Logic of Women on Trial: Case Studies of Popular American Trials.* Carbondale, IL: Southern Illinois University Press, 1994.

Spierling, Frank. *Lizzie.* New York: Random House, 1984.

Weinberg, Kenneth G. *A Man's Home, A Man's Castle.* New York: McCall Publishing Company, 1971.

Whipple, Sidney B. *The Trial of Bruno Richard Hauptmann.* Garden City, NY: Doubleday, Doran and Company, 1937.

Title Index

An Arrogant Man: The Trial of David C. Stephenson, Grand Dragon of the Ku Klux Klan, 89

Evading the Truth: The United States of America vs. Al Capone, 117

A Deadly Secret: The Lincoln Assassination Conspiracy Trial, 1

In Defense of Home: The People of Michigan vs. Ossian Sweet et al., 103

A Perfect Crime: The People against Nathan Leopold, Jr. and Richard Loeb: The Sentencing Hearing, 59

"Say It Ain't So": The State of Illinois vs. Eddie Cicotte et al., 43

She Took an Axe . . . : The Commonwealth of Massachusetts vs. Lizzie Borden, 25

Taking the Test: The State of Tennessee vs. John Thomas Scopes, 71

When the Bough Breaks: The State vs. Hauptmann, 135

A Woman's Right: The United States vs. Susan B. Anthony, 13

About the Author

Suzanne I. Barchers is Editor in Chief/Vice President of LeapFrog's Schoolhouse Division. She also serves on the board of directors for the Association of Educational Publishers (EdPress) and as consulting editor for Teacher Ideas Press, which is part of the Greenwood Publishing Group. She has a doctorate in curriculum and has written numerous articles and twenty books for the education market, including readers theatre, cookbooks, and college textbooks. Other writing projects include more than twenty children's books for Leapfrog's school and trade divisions, a CD-ROM, and a music curriculum. Previous positions include managing editor at *Weekly Reader*, Editorial Director for Fulcrum Publishing's Resource and Children's books, and part-time teaching at the University of Colorado at Denver.